Preaching without Contempt

Other Titles in
Fortress Resources for Preaching

⁓

Preaching without Contempt

Overcoming
Unintended Anti-Judaism

Marilyn J. Salmon

Fortress Press
Minneapolis

3-14-23

PREACHING WITHOUT CONTEMPT
Overcoming Unintended Anti-Judaism

Library of Congress Cataloging-in-Publication Data
Salmon, Marilyn J.
  Preaching without contempt : overcoming unintended anti-Judaism / Marilyn J. Salmon.
    p. cm.
  ISBN 0-8006-3821-2 (alk. paper)
  1. Judaism (Christian theology). 2. Christianity and antisemitism. 3. Preaching. I. Title.
  BT93.S25 2006
  261.2'6—dc22

                                    2005035400

10   09   08   07   06   1   2   3   4   5   6   7   8   9   10

For my sons,

Jesse and Isaac

∼

Contents

Preface

THIS BOOK IS FOR preachers who think it is not for them. They think it is not for them because they would never *knowingly* say anything overtly negative about Jews or Judaism. It is for Christians who formally reject supersessionism, honor the validity of modern Judaism, and take critical biblical interpretation seriously, but who nevertheless wonder—or even suspect—that elements of anti-Jewish prejudice and stereotypes may nonetheless linger in their preaching. It is for conscientious church leaders responsible for programs, pastoral care, and administration, in addition to preaching and worship, who cannot afford to spend valuable time reading a book they presume they do not need. This book is for preachers who think the topic of anti-Judaism is irrelevant because they serve in rural areas where there is no Jewish population and therefore they have no contact with Judaism.

Even the most conscientious preachers unknowingly rely on stereotypes of Judaism. They do not do so intentionally, but the negative portrayals of Jews are so familiar they do not recognize them as a form of anti-Judaism. Caricatures of Judaism are so deeply ingrained in Christian tradition it is difficult to recognize them for what they are: a creation of early Christian apologetics to show the superiority of Christianity. Preachers repeat them, unaware of their origin, and thus unwittingly perpetuate the long history of Christian anti-Judaism.

This book is intended also for seminary classrooms where students first learn the fundamentals of biblical exegesis and the art of preaching. Here, where future lay and ordained church leaders learn to relate theory and practice, is a prime place to develop an awareness of Christian anti-Judaism and why it is important to learn to recognize and overcome it.

This book is also for people who listen to sermons and are hurt by what they hear. They have Jewish spouses, or nieces, or neighbors, or friends, and they are offended to hear Jewish customs trivialized or Jesus' contemporaries ridiculed. And it is for people who are not offended by what they hear. I hope that Christian educators will find the book useful to generate conversations about Judaism, anti-Judaism, and biblical interpretation. I hope it helps train our ears to hear the offense.

The purpose of this book is to raise awareness of the negative images of Judaism that commonly occur in preaching, to learn to recognize them, and to adopt strategies to avoid repeating them. One could be deceived by how simple this sounds. First, because caricatures of Jews and Judaism are deeply ingrained in Christian tradition, they are thus a familiar and habitual part of Christian preaching. Second, the resources for preaching reinforce stereotypes of Judaism. The Christian Scriptures present negative portrayals of Jews, particularly in the description of Jesus' adversaries in the Gospels. Lectionaries often pair readings to imply that Christianity superseded an inferior Judaism. Commentaries and favorite theologies also reflect the deeply formed Christian prejudices against Judaism in both subtle and not-so-subtle ways. It is therefore not surprising that well-intended preachers nevertheless use familiar forms of anti-Judaism in sermons.

The focus in this book is on the Gospels because they are the most common sources for sermons, and because contrasting Jesus over and against his Jewish contemporaries and the customs of his day is the most pervasive kind of unintended anti-Judaism. The Gospels themselves sound anti-Jewish. However, I maintain they are not. The Gospels belong *within* the context of first-century Judaism. They were written before Christianity existed apart from Judaism. We read the Gospels differently when we think of them as Jewish literature rather than Christian literature, written by Christians about Jews. This insight is critical for Christians who regularly move from Gospel text to sermon. Furthermore, a basic knowledge of the diversity of first-century Judaism is critical for interpreting the Gospels.

Simply learning about Judaism does not automatically translate into the elimination of anti-Judaism in preaching. For that reason,

I include examples from sermons to help readers become conscious of common unintended stereotypes. Included also are examples from sermons that overcome negative portrayals of Jews to show alternatives to the temptation to rely on traditional negative images. Admittedly, it can be an effective homiletical device to contrast Jesus with blind, rigid, hypocritical Pharisees to make a point! The aim is not to help preachers prepare sermons about Judaism, but rather to help us avoid habitual misrepresentations of Judaism in sermons week after week.

A secondary purpose closely connected to removing anti-Judaism is proclaiming the Christian gospel without depending on an "other." I believe that one of the reasons we continue to depend on a deficient form of Judaism is because it effectively displays the superiority of Christianity. But I am convinced that the best preaching does not need to create an "us" and "them" to be effective. Christianity does not need an inferior Judaism to support the truth of the gospel. Jesus does not need misguided adversaries to improve his image. Christianity is compelling on its own terms. It is my hope that working toward eliminating contempt for Judaism will have the effect of eliminating contempt for any "other" as a rhetorical device.

I use some terms in the book that may be new to the reader. I use the terms *Older Testament* and *Newer Testament* for the two parts of the Christian Scriptures rather than *Old* and *New Testament* as a way to diminish implied supersessionism. I retain the more familiar terms *Old Testament* and *New Testament* when describing more traditional interpretations. I also distinguish between the Christian Older Testament and the Tanak of Judaism. While these terms refer to *nearly* identical writings, the two religious communities have distinct histories of interpretation. This is a way to remind Christian readers that these writings stand on their own in Judaism, without a New Testament. Readers may observe that I often use the title *Messiah* for Jesus where they expect the more familiar *Christ*. I do so to emphasize the Jewish context of early claims about Jesus and to reinforce the identification of *Christ* with *Messiah*. The title *Christ* comes to us through the Greek translation of the Hebrew term for *Messiah*. Other terms that may be unfamiliar or take on distinctive meanings will be explained as they occur in the discussion.

Acknowledgments

Writing this book has not been a solo enterprise. The preface affords the opportunity to express gratitude to many for support. I am grateful to United Theological Seminary for making possible a half-year sabbatical to get the project underway, for research assistance, and for the encouragement from faculty colleagues. Paul Capetz, Mary Bednarowski, and Chris Smith read all or parts of the manuscript, providing valuable insights and catching a few inaccuracies. Thanks to research assistants Deirdre Hinz and Shirley Koepsel who combed the Internet and journals for sermon illustrations. Pam Wynn provided professional, skilled proofreading and editing, thus improving immeasurably the final manuscript. Fortress Press editor-in-chief Michael West's positive response to my proposal provided motivation along the way when progress was slow. And thanks to Neil Elliott and the editorial team, who guided the process from manuscript to book. I am grateful likewise for St. Clement's Episcopal Church, for the rector, The Rev. Daniel Pearson, who shared the pulpit with me, and for the people who have listened to my sermons. It is a wonderful place to preach.

This book is written to honor the memory of Marcia Yugend, a gifted and tireless bridge-builder between Jews and Christians. She created ways for us to talk to each other openly and respectfully. Her sudden death in 1999 left a void in the dialogue between Jews and Christians in our communities as well as in the lives of her family and friends. She was a strong advocate for reading biblical texts together. I have been particularly mindful of Marcia while writing this book and often wished I could share it with her. I am grateful for her inspiration.

I dedicate this book also to my sons, Jesse and Isaac, with the hope that one day they will wonder why writing it seemed important.

Introduction

AT UNITED THEOLOGICAL SEMINARY, I teach a class called "Interpreting the Bible after the Holocaust." Students generally embrace enthusiastically the principles of the course and by the end of the term easily recognize some of the ways anti-Jewish themes appear in biblical interpretation. I was dismayed, therefore, when an exceptionally insightful student delivered a chapel sermon in which he relied on a historically inaccurate portrayal of Judaism as a foil to demonstrate superior Christian values. In just the previous term in his final exam he had written a fine essay showing his knowledge of first-century Judaism as well as his ability to apply what he knew to interpreting Newer Testament texts. When I asked the student about the disparity between his excellent exam and the just-preached sermon, he, too, was dismayed. He was not at all conscious of what he had done in his sermon.

This is not an unusual occurrence. I devote a considerable time in the Newer Testament introduction courses to early Judaism, the historical Pharisees, the Gospels as Jewish literature, and Jewish and Christian origins. I am frequently perplexed by the disjuncture between class and chapel. This experience is not limited to student preachers and seminary chapel. I hear experienced preachers rely on anti-Jewish biases to make a point, clergy who likely would be appalled by the suggestion that their sermons contained anything construed as anti-Jewish. This is less a criticism than a question.

What accounts for the inconsistency between classroom and pulpit? Why do preachers knowledgeable about first-century Judaism rely on the anti-Jewish stereotypes of Christian tradition? Why do clergy who profess commitment to interfaith relations preach sermons that include contempt for Judaism? I also ponder why

preachers trained in historical-critical methods of biblical interpretation often appear not to apply these methods to the practice
of preaching. I believe there are several reasons that may account
for the disjuncture between "theory and practice." The nature of
preaching may account for apparent contradictions between knowledge and practical application. Biblical literature also lends itself to
using Jews and Judaism as a foil to display "superior" Christianity.
Perhaps the greatest obstacle is that biased stereotypes of Judaism
are so deeply ingrained in Christian tradition.

The Nature of Preaching

The purpose of a sermon in the context of Christian worship is
to proclaim the gospel of Jesus Christ. A sermon usually contains
didactic elements, but that is not its primary function. While a
preacher may choose to use the sermon to teach on a particular
theme or issue, nevertheless, the goal is to illumine the Christian
gospel. In other words, the sermon is not a lecture. Classroom learning and exegetical skills do not automatically translate to delivering
an effective sermon.

The sermon is occasional in nature, shaped by the liturgical season, the biblical readings, the worship customs, and the makeup of
the listeners. Biblical preaching requires the preacher to "preach the
text" as it relates to a certain set of circumstances. When I prepare
to preach, I am aware of a wide range of human experiences and
dispositions in the congregation and the possible effect of my words
on the feminist, the newcomer, the Republican, the Democrat, the
recently divorced, the just-widowed, the new parents, the dying, and
so forth. How do the biblical readings for the day relate to the situation, including the diversity of experiences individuals bring to the
occasion as well as the collective identity of the community? It is
very rare that I preach the same sermon in my church and the seminary chapel, even when I use the same biblical readings.

And, according to current norms with which I am familiar, the
sermon is short. In Christian denominations with a sacramental
and formal liturgical tradition, the sermon, or homily, is limited
to twelve to fifteen minutes. Thus, a sermon typically develops a
single idea or makes a single point that relates Christian faith to
human experience. I was trained to craft a three-point sermon,

but I can't remember when I last heard one. The art of preaching has changed.

Given the purpose of the sermon and the occasional nature of preaching, there are many demands on the preacher. She must proclaim the gospel, relate it to the lives of the listeners in a limited amount of time, and also conform to the customs of the worship service. It is therefore not so surprising that attention to the matter of anti-Jewish stereotypes may not receive a high priority.

Liabilities of the Biblical Texts

Biblical texts that serve as the basis for the sermon often create a stumbling block for preachers, even those who are in other circumstances sensitive to traditional Christian portrayals of Judaism. The lectionaries (Roman Catholic, Lutheran, Episcopalian, and the Revised Common Lectionary used by clergy in several Protestant denominations) often pair readings from the Older Testament and the Gospels that reinforce anti-Jewish themes. And the polemical texts in the Gospels certainly sound anti-Jewish. The biblical literature seems to set the preacher up to perpetuate biased stereotypes, even when one is aware and intellectually committed to counteract them.

For example, on the Fourth Sunday of Advent, the lectionaries in Cycle A pair Isa. 7:10-14 and Matt. 1:18-25. The selections seem obvious, since the author of Matthew quotes Isa. 7:14. (Well, not exactly! Careful readers and listeners observe that Isaiah refers to a "young woman" and Matthew's quotation says "virgin." This difference can be attributed to the author of Matthew's use of the Septuagint, which has translated the Hebrew word for "young woman" with the Greek for "virgin." Very perceptive readers and listeners will notice that, according to Isaiah, the mother names the child, while according to Matthew, "they" call the child, named Jesus by his parents, Immanuel.) But the juxtaposition of these texts on that Sunday reinforces an uncritical and traditional Christian view that the prophet Isaiah literally foretold the birth of Jesus in the eighth century B.C.E. This understanding of prophecy in effect denies any meaning the prophecy had in its eighth-century context or for the communities of faith that recorded and handed down the prophetic literature to succeeding generations. It also implies that the identity of Jesus should have been obvious to all since the prophets predicted the circumstances of his birth.

A similar prophecy-fulfillment pairing occurs in Cycle B on the Second Sunday of Advent. Mark 1:1-8 cites Isa. 40:3 and applies it to John the Baptist, leading Christian listeners to conclude that Isaiah prophesied the role of John the Baptist as a forerunner to Jesus Messiah. Another occurs on Christmas Eve/Day each year when the lectionaries assign the familiar prophecy of Isaiah 9 for the first reading: "For a child has been born to us, a son given to us." And on Good Friday the lectionaries select Isaiah 52, one of the Suffering Servant Songs, which to Christian ears is a quite explicit foretelling of Jesus' suffering and death.

A preacher may recognize that the author of Mark adjusts the Hebrew parallelism to make the citation from Isaiah work. (Isaiah 40:3 reads, "A voice cries out: 'In the wilderness prepare the way of the Lord, make straight in the desert a highway for our God,'" whereas Mark reads, "*the* voice of one crying in the wilderness: 'Prepare the way of the LORD, make his paths straight.'") A seminary-educated preacher likely knows about the several interpretations of the Suffering Servant Songs of Isaiah. Most may reject a literal interpretation of the Older Testament prophecies as predicting the birth and suffering and death of Jesus. And some might view the Gospel writers as interpreters of their Scriptures (which later became our Older Testament) in the way they manipulate the texts, and not as careless or inaccurate transmitters. But if they remember what they learned and what they claim to believe, this may not be evident in their sermons on these occasions. Given the expectations of the liturgical seasons of Advent, Christmas, and Holy Week in Lent, and with echoes of Handel's *Messiah* in the air, these are not occasions that lend themselves to a didactic sermon on the nature of biblical prophecy or the historical context of either the Older Testament prophecies or the late first-century settings of the Gospels. Yet, when we read these Older and Newer Testament passages together and at these times in the church year, the effect is to reinforce the common themes of Christian anti-Judaism: the sole purpose of the Old Testament is to point to the New Testament, specifically to Jesus; the New Testament supersedes the Old Testament, and Christianity replaces Judaism as the New Israel; Jews did not (and do not) understand their own Scriptures. I add here that even if the preacher selects biblical readings rather than follows a lectionary, these texts are the most likely choices for these occasions in the church year. People expect to hear them. These are biblical passages with which they are familiar, and they associate them with the seasons.[1]

There are other instances of lectionary pairings that reinforce the Christian preaching of contempt for Judaism, but these demonstrate the problem for the preacher who is committed to historically accurate and more favorable portrayals of Judaism yet neglects the matter or gives it a low priority in light of other considerations. The lectionary selections are not responsible, though, for the fact that the Gospel pericopes themselves present obstacles for the preacher who is otherwise sensitive to anti-Jewish themes.

In a class on interpreting the Gospels, a student presented a good exegesis on a pericope pitting the Pharisees against Jesus, taking into account the groups within early Judaism in the latter part of the first century and a historically sound description of the Pharisees. When I asked how she might preach it, she cast the Pharisees as representing unfavorable characteristics as a contrast to the admirable qualities of Jesus. When I pointed out the contradiction between exegesis and preaching ideas, she replied, "Well, I would never choose this to preach on." I replied, "Then what *will* you preach on?"

Controversies between Jesus and the Pharisees, the Jewish authorities, and narratives critical of Jewish customs permeate the Gospels. There is no way to avoid them. And they work so well! The controversies lend themselves easily to extol Christian virtues over against inferior Judaism. This approach is so familiar in Christian tradition—the so-called preaching of contempt—preachers are usually unaware that they have misrepresented first-century Judaism and, by implication, contemporary Judaism. So deeply ingrained is the tendency to read the Gospels over against Jews and Judaism that the caricatures surface even when they are absent from the text. For example, in a sermon I heard recently, the homilist asserted that the Pharisees had long ago abandoned the concept of love for neighbor and that Jews cared only about the rituals of the Temple. The Gospel upon which she based the homily made no mention of Pharisees or Jews or Temple rituals, however. I don't think it is uncommon to read such caricatures into the text whether they are present explicitly or not.

The Gospels do sound anti-Jewish. But are they? Some scholars think that they are, that the Gospel writers introduced their hostility toward Judaism into the Gospel narratives. Others disagree. I am convinced that the polemic of the Gospels reflects intra-Jewish debates prior to the schism between Judaism and Christianity. The problem of anti-Judaism is a matter of interpretation and not intrinsic to the Gospels. The Gospels were Jewish literature, written by and for Jews within the context of the diversity of first-century Judaism. In the first chapter, I will show that the Gospels belong within Judaism. A premise of this book is that interpreting the Gospels within the context of the diversity of early Judaism will help the preacher counter anti-Jewish stereotypes in sermons.

First-Century Judaism and Twenty-First-Century Judaism

Christians often do not perceive a connection between first-century Judaism and their Jewish neighbors. So, a minister may be committed to Jewish-Christian relations in her community yet not be concerned with negative portrayals of first-century Judaism in sermons. But they are intimately related.

I once suggested that a preacher who takes the portrayal of the Pharisees in the Newer Testament as a historical description, casting them as legalistic, hypocritical, and as committed to the letter of the Law, implies that these were and *are* characteristics of Judaism. A listener looked puzzled. "But the Pharisees don't have anything to do with Judaism today." I disagreed, pointing out that modern Judaism traces its origins to second-century Rabbinic Judaism, which developed out of Pharisaism, similar to the way Christians locate their origins in the mission of Jesus and the preaching of the apostles, out of which developed Christianity in the second century.[2] Most Christians, I believe, would be offended if someone, especially an outsider, maligned the apostles, let alone Jesus. We are not first-century Christians, but the stories of Jesus and the Epistles, especially Paul's, inform our Christian faith and belief and our identity as Christians. The role of the Pharisees is not precisely the same for Jews, but it plays an important role in the origin of Rabbinic Judaism. A demeaning portrayal of the Pharisees denigrates modern Judaism.

As indicated above, preachers may support Christian supersessionism, the view that Christianity replaced Judaism as heir of the promises of God to Israel, in the ways they relate the two

Christian testaments. Some common assumptions are that the laws of the Old Testament are no longer valid with the arrival of the Messiah; that Old Testament prophesies are fulfilled in the New Testament; and that the God of wrath is different from the God of love in the New Testament (incredibly still quite common in the pew if not in the pulpit). A skeptic, who doubted that what preachers said about the Old Testament had anything to do with Jews today, claimed, "My Jewish friends don't live according to the Old Testament!" No. And yes. Jews today do not live literally according to the *Tanak* (the Jewish name for their Scriptures, an acronym from the first Hebrew letter of Torah, Prophets, and Writings, the three parts of the Jewish Bible), not even fundamentalists. But observant Jews—Reform, Conservative, Reconstructionist, Orthodox alike—do look to the *Tanak* and the history of rabbinic interpretation to inform their practice of Judaism. When we limit the Christian Older Testament to its place in Christian salvation history, we dismiss the long history of Jewish interpretation and the place of the *Tanak* in modern Judaism. The *Tanak* and Older Testament are shared Scriptures, but Christians and Jews interpret them differently.

The questioners who doubted a connection between the Pharisees or the Older Testament and modern Judaism based their perceptions on experience with Jewish friends and colleagues. They do not know them to be legalistic hypocrites or enslaved to antiquated laws. For them and others who have Jewish friends and neighbors, their experience takes precedence over negative portrayals of first-century Jews. But even among these there may be little knowledge of Jewish religious customs or the foundations of Judaism. This is not necessarily a common topic of conversation among colleagues and casual friends. Many Christians, however, have little or no opportunity for contact with Judaism. Christian tradition along with Western culture informs perceptions of Judaism.

I hear presumptions from seminary students, in adult education classes, and in clergy groups, too, indicating that perceptions of Jewish life today are largely determined by what they have learned about first-century Judaism in a Christian context: "I thought Jews believed . . ."; "But Jews are still waiting for . . ."; "Jews reject. . . ." What we have learned is a construction of first-century Judaism that serves the purposes of displaying the origin of Christianity to advantage and projects this view of Jews and Judaism into the twenty-first century. Preachers who assume that negative portrayals of Jews in the first century have nothing to do with misrepresentations of Judaism in the twenty-first century are mistaken. It is impossible to cast first-century Judaism as deficient without implying that the same flaws exist in Judaism today.

Default Literalism

I surmise that there is a tendency among busy preachers, given the nature of sermonizing, to fall back on a literal reading of the Gospel texts. I know clergy who can and do give learned lectures on historical-Jesus studies, who apply biblical criticism to illuminate texts related to contemporary issues, but who in sermons give the impression that the biblical narratives are accurate historical documents, or resort to uncritical, familiar readings of texts. For example, when the preacher asserts what Jesus said or did, or what Jesus thought, or what he opposed, he confirms the perception that we are hearing a historical account of what happened one day in the life of Jesus. I recognize that it may be awkward to avoid this, but if one consistently conveys the idea that the Gospels give us a literal account of the ministry of Jesus, then they also provide a historically reliable picture of the Pharisees and other Jews in the time of Jesus. For example, I read a sermon in a diocesan Web site in which the preacher assailed the faults of biblical literalism in contrast to Jesus' own nonliteral scriptural interpretations that were unique among his contemporaries! The effect of this default literalism inevitably perpetuates anti-Jewish stereotypes already so deeply ingrained in Christian consciousness.

Summary

There are several factors that undermine a preacher's best intentions with respect to the problem of misrepresenting Jews and Judaism in sermons. The minister must consider first of all that the purpose of a sermon is proclamation. A sermon is occasional in nature, and so the preacher must take into account the particulars of context, such as liturgical season, lectionary readings (or those selected for the occasion), and the character and concerns of the congregation. There is also the constraint of time, time allowed for the sermon itself as well as the realistic limits on the pastor's time for preparation. Further, there are obstacles one encounters in biblical texts. For homilists who follow a lectionary, the lectionary pairings often reinforce biased Christian views of Judaism. Controversies between Jesus and the Pharisees and other Jews present another challenge. Indeed, the perceived anti-Jewish character of the Gospels undermines the efforts of any well-intentioned preacher who desires to put into practice an enlightened understanding of Jews and Judaism. The tendency to resort to a familiar literalism or to rationalize a discontinuity between the Judaism of the time of Jesus and modern Judaism is perhaps understandable. The challenges make theological and ethical commitments difficult to carry out.

I advocate, nevertheless, that preachers give high priority to eliminating anti-Judaism in their sermons. In spite of the obstacles and limitations that may inhibit preachers from putting their theological views and biblical interpretation skills into practice, there are ethical and pastoral reasons for treating this matter with great seriousness. It is my conviction that relying on caricatures created to advance Christianity at the expense of Judaism or using Jewish stereotypes as a foil to elevate Christian virtues is contrary to the Christian gospel and has no place in Christian preaching. My purpose here is to propose a hermeneutic and strategies for faithfully proclaiming the gospel without perpetuating the centuries-old Christian tradition of the preaching of contempt against Judaism.

The Ethics of Preaching after the Holocaust

Christians are not responsible for the Holocaust. Nazis are responsible for first denying Jews the rights of other citizens, taking away their livelihood and property, putting them in ghettoes, then concentration camps, and conceiving the Final Solution. Nazis are liable for the murder of six million Jews in addition to countless homosexuals, gypsies, the handicapped, and political resisters. Certainly there were Christians who were Nazis, but Christianity itself is not responsible for the Holocaust.

Christianity is culpable, however, for creating the environment that made the Holocaust possible. For centuries, since Constantine converted to Christianity and made it the religion of the Roman Empire, Christians have oppressed, persecuted, and murdered Jews in the name of Christianity. They were incited against Jews by the preaching of contempt they heard in their churches. Jews were charged with deicide, with rejecting God's Messiah, disobedience against God for rejecting the truth of their own Scriptures. That was how the church interpreted its Scriptures. Sadly, that is our history with respect to Judaism.

The church has a long history of anti-Judaism, that is, a prejudice against the religion of the Jews. In theory, at least, if a Jew were baptized and converted to Christianity, he or she would no longer be the object of contempt. Anti-Semitism, on the other hand, is racial bigotry. The Third Reich created a pseudo-scientific racial profile of Jews and sought to exterminate Jews as a race. But again, Christian anti-Judaism is the context in which anti-Semitism emerged. In the Western world, Christian culture classified Jews as inferior, limited their participation in society, and at times persecuted and murdered them. It is a small step from Christian anti-Judaism to the anti-Semitism of Hitler's Third Reich. To put it bluntly, anti-Judaism made anti-Semitism possible.[3] So, while Christianity alone is not responsible for the Holocaust, neither is it absolved from all guilt.

James Carroll, in his book *Constantine's Sword,* surveys the history of the Roman Catholic Church (which *is* the church for most of Christian history in the West) in its relationship with Judaism. His premise is that things could have been different. He demonstrates that the Church made decisions, choosing one theological perspective over another that affected Jews adversely, or preferring a biblical interpretation that undermined Judaism at the expense of superior Christianity.[4] In other words, Christianity is not at its core, in its very origin, inevitably anti-Jewish. Our Scriptures are not intrinsically anti-Jewish, and Christian theology need not be anti-Jewish. Christians historically bear responsibility for framing an orthodoxy that hurt Jews over many centuries. But Christians in this century are not constrained by their decisions. We can be intentional in our theological and biblical interpretation with respect to our relationship with Jews and Judaism and mindful of what we say in sermons, so that the long history of contempt might come to an end in our own time. We are ethically bound to do so.

Christianity must not remain unchanged after the Holocaust. Christian scholarship has responded to the ethical imperative dictated by Christianity's history of anti-Judaism and complicity in the Shoah. Theologians have constructed systematic theologies that respond intentionally to the historical bias against Judaism.[5] Biblical scholars have offered new interpretations of Paul and the Gospels within Judaism rather than over against it.[6] Some have given specific attention to problematic texts with respect to Judaism.[7] A survey of book titles published in the last two decades indicates a significant interest in the subject of the Jewishness of Jesus, Christianity in relation to Judaism, and first-century Judaism. My intent here is to relate current biblical scholarship with respect to Judaism to the practice of biblical preaching. At stake is the ethics of Christian proclamation.

Pastoral Issues

Clergy who serve congregations generally have some idea of who their listeners are and they preach with a pastoral sensitivity to those present. We also can and do assume that most of those present at worship are Christians or open to hearing the Christian Gospel. These circumstances make it easy to overlook the matter of how we present Jews and Judaism in sermons, or this may simply get lost in the midst of more evident pastoral concerns. In fact, however, we never know for sure who will be among our listeners.

I attended a funeral in a small church in a small town in a rural area where one probably could count the number of Jews in the surrounding counties on one's fingers. The absence of a Jewish presence here no doubt makes the issue of Christian anti-Judaism seem remote. But one of the children of the deceased had married a Jew, so a Jewish spouse, Jewish children, grandchildren, and in-laws occupied the first two pews. The pastor had a little time to think about Scripture readings and prayers and a sermon that would be sensitive to family members without diminishing the proclamation of Christian faith in the resurrection. But if one has habitually dismissed the relevance of forms of anti-Judaism, one will not be sufficiently alert to how and where they occur, as sadly happened on this occasion. The pastor certainly did not intend to offend, but he did, and he missed an opportunity for pastoral care for the whole family.

Developing a sensitivity to aspects of anti-Judaism requires consciousness-raising and hearing with "other" ears. How will this sound to a Jewish person? Or the Christian spouse of a Jew? Or child? Or friend? In large urban areas where interaction between Jews and Christians is more likely, one risks offending parishioners and visitors in attendance. At a service that was to include a baptism, I was surprised to see several Jewish friends who had been invited to attend the service by the parents of a child to be baptized. After greeting them, I mentally went through the service and remembered that the Gospel for the day was from John 20, beginning with verse 19: ". . . the doors of the house . . . were locked for fear of the Jews." When I read the Gospel, I replaced "Jews" with "Judeans." I could not imagine reading the text as it is translated in the NRSV and thereby offending our guests. In this passage, translating "Judeans" indicates the fear is of a people living in a geographical area rather than fear of a religious kind. (A few modern translations render *Ioudaioi* as Judeans in this passage.)

Amy-Jill Levine, a Jewish scholar who teaches New Testament at Vanderbilt, tells about bringing her young son to class, seating him in front of the students, and admonishing them, "Don't you dare say anything in your sermons that would hurt this child!"[8] Imagining a Jewish presence in the congregation is a good way to hear your sermon with other ears and avoid reliance on familiar anti-Jewish stereotypes in preaching.

A second pastoral issue concerns the obligation on the part of pastoral leaders to give their congregants their very best. I imagine that most readers of this book have, or are going to have, a theological education. Most mainstream denominations require it, indicating that they value a theologically educated clergy. The "people in the pew" expect their pastoral leaders to put it to use. They probably do not want to be told what they know, but they do want them to apply their education, to put it into practice.

In a class with a large number of new students I had just introduced an interpretation of the apostle Paul that challenged the cherished views of some. A student professed that she was okay with this but added, "I would never preach this in a congregation; they just couldn't handle it." I couldn't resist pointing out that until a few months ago she was in the pew with the people who just couldn't handle it, and she seemed to be doing okay. There is some truth to the student's perception, however, that people will find new interpretations challenging and that they don't want to be challenged. Who does? It's uncomfortable. We prefer to be comforted and supported. And parish leaders want to be liked and affirmed. We know, though, that the gospel both afflicts and affirms. Authentic proclamation of the Christian gospel will both challenge as well as comfort. Faithfulness to our vocation as preachers requires that we put our theological education into practice with those whom we serve.

Conclusion

My purpose here is first to raise awareness of how preachers perpetuate Christian anti-Judaism in sermons. I believe it is unintentional, but the images of Judaism are so familiar that clergy and laity alike don't hear the slander in casting the Pharisees as hypocritically legalistic, or contrasting the letter of the Law in Judaism with the spirit of the Law represented by Jesus, or in ascribing to early Judaism the opposite of Christian virtues. The first step toward eliminating anti-Jewish bias is consciousness-raising so that we become accustomed to recognizing it. Then when one prepares to preach it simply will be part of one's consciousness and not the burden of one more thing to remember.

My emphasis here is on the canonical Gospels. I have chosen this focus for a number of reasons. In the first place, teaching and preaching the Gospels is my vocation. I teach the Gospels in a Christian seminary and preach regularly in an Episcopal church. I received my seminary education at a Lutheran seminary and as preparation for ordination as an Episcopal priest I took additional classes at an Episcopal seminary. In both of these traditions preaching on the Gospel reading appointed by the lectionary is customary practice, though not mandatory, and a practice shared by most who follow a lectionary. But even if one does not follow a lectionary, the Gospel stories of Jesus hold a privileged place in Christian proclamation. The stories lend themselves to preaching. Form criticism has shown that they originated in the preaching and teaching of the early church. They also are potent sources for the preaching of contempt.

In the following chapters I will describe the prominent themes in the long history of the preaching of contempt and cite selected texts that traditionally support them. I will offer suggestions for reinterpretation and strategies for countering anti-Jewish stereotypes and for correcting assumptions about Judaism when we read passages that sound anti-Jewish. Chapters include sermons, or passages from sermons, to illustrate ways to handle problem texts without compromising the intended message the preacher plans for the sermon.

Chapter 1, "The Gospels as Jewish Literature," provides a basic introduction to early Judaism and places the Gospels within the context of the diversity of Judaism in the first century. Using primary sources, I show that the Gospels were, at the time they were written in the last third of the first century, Jewish literature. They were written before Christianity existed apart from Judaism; the authors were Jews writing for a predominantly Jewish audience in the midst of the process of identity formation following the destruction of the Temple in 70 C.E. Given this context, we read the Gospel narratives, especially controversies, as intra-Jewish rather than Jews versus Christians. I think that a more reliable historical construction of Judaism and considering the Newer Testament literature within the context of first-century Judaism will help the preacher avoid contrasting Christianity as superior to Judaism.

Chapter 2 focuses on Christian supersessionism. The concept that Christianity replaced Judaism as heir of the promises of God to Israel is pervasive in the way we read our Scriptures. The question here is how to be true to our Christian faith without demeaning the faith of others. Having already begun to address this matter with a reconstruction of Christian origins within the context of the diversity of early Judaism in chapter 1, in this chapter, I give examples of how supersessionism is expressed, often unintentionally, through very common readings of Gospel texts. The most conspicuous incidences of Christian supersessionism are in the ways we relate the two testaments of our Bible. I emphasize the continuity between the Older and Newer Testaments rather than discontinuity and difference. I include in this chapter some strategies for interpreting these continuities in a way that honors the integrity of Judaism as well as authentic Christian faith. I believe that Christianity need not define itself over against Judaism; to continue to do so is a misuse of the Scriptures.

Chapter 3 deals with the Pharisees and the Law. The Gospels frequently present the Pharisees as opponents of Jesus and give a generally unflattering, even hostile, portrayal of them, and Christians have accepted this portrait as historically accurate. Drawing from primary sources, I offer a definition of the Pharisees that is historically reliable and give some ways of interpreting the polemic against the Pharisees in the Gospels. I also show that the Newer Testament does not uniformly portray the Pharisees as opponents; there are exceptions.

Closely linked to the stereotype of the Pharisees as hypocritically legalistic is a Christian ambivalence toward the Law. The concept that the early Christians' rejection of the Mosaic Law was one of the reasons for the schism between Judaism and Christianity figures prominently in conventional views of Christian origins. Contrasting the letter of the Law with the spirit of the Law is another way Christians have distanced themselves from Jewish observance. The Gospels actually take the Law very seriously. In this chapter, I both suggest that Christians must reconsider the supposition that the Gospels oppose Torah observance and also correct the caricature of the Pharisees.

I devote all of chapter 4 to the Gospel of John because this Gospel presents special problems with respect to anti-Judaism. The controversies in the Synoptic Gospels become harsh polemic against "the Jews" in the Fourth Gospel and make it difficult to hear it as anything but a condemnation of Jews and Judaism. Scholars differ on the subject of this Gospel and anti-Judaism.[9] Some conclude that the author of John did indeed harbor hostile feelings toward Judaism. Some scholars detect strata in the Gospel coming from different contexts, an earlier one from within Judaism, the last separate from and opposed to Judaism. Others place the writing of this Gospel pre-schism, representing a group of believers marginalized from the local synagogue because of their claims about Jesus. I am in agreement with the latter perspective. In this chapter, I suggest that reading John as sectarian literature helps the interpreter understand the harsh polemic in its late first-century context as other than anti-Jewish.

The Passion narrative merits special attention in a separate chapter because of its unique role in Christian history for fostering hatred toward Jews and because of its central place in Christian faith and identity. The narratives in the Gospels include both events that are historically reliable, such as the crucifixion of Jesus, along with Christian apologetics concerning responsibility for his death and the meaning of his death and resurrection. The charge of deicide comes from the Gospel narratives and their depiction in art and dramatization in Passion plays. Anti-Judaism emerges not only in sermons but from simply reading the Gospel narrative during the holiest week of the Christian calendar. In this chapter I discuss the importance of interpreting the Passion narrative within the context of early Judaism and of addressing the matter of historicity.

I am sympathetic to the challenges of interpreting ancient sacred texts in the form of a sermon or homily that faithfully proclaims the gospel in a way that is relevant to the lives of contemporary Christian listeners. One of these challenges is to counter the long tradition of "teaching contempt," the reading of Christian Scriptures over against Judaism. The negative portrayals of Jews and Judaism are so deeply ingrained in our history and experience that we quite often do not hear or recognize them. My purpose in the chapters that follow is to raise the level of consciousness with respect to the anti-Jewish stereotypes that frequently emerge in sermons and to provide some strategies toward preaching without contempt for Judaism in the proclamation of the Christian Gospel.

1

The Gospels as Jewish Literature

WHEN I BEGAN TEACHING, a former teacher asked me if I taught any courses on Judaism. "Yes," I replied. "All of them." He nodded and smiled, though most would find my response a bit puzzling. I teach Newer Testament courses. The Newer Testament belongs to Christianity, a religion with a long history separate from Judaism. But my point, in my admittedly tongue-in-cheek response, was that the literature of the Newer Testament, at the time it was written in the first century C.E., belonged to early Judaism. The literature, from the perspective of author and audience, was Jewish literature.

Christians have a very long history of reading the letters of Paul and the Gospels while assuming that the schism between Judaism and Christianity had already occurred, and that Jesus himself stood apart from his Jewish heritage. From this point of view, Christianity was the antithesis of Judaism; Judaism represented the opposite of whatever defined Christianity. So, if Paul asserted salvation by grace apart from the works of the Law, then Jews must have believed in salvation on the basis of works of the Law. When Jesus bent or broke Sabbath law, Jesus represented the spirit of the Law in contrast to the rigid letter of the Law of Judaism. The Newer Testament writings depict Christianity's openness to Gentiles, thereby rejecting Judaism's closed ethnocentrism.

A shift has occurred in scholarship in the last few decades. Pauline scholars, both Jews and Christians, who situate the Apostle Paul within Judaism prior to the schism between Judaism and Christianity, dominate Pauline studies. Scholarship on the Gospels has also undergone a paradigm shift. The Gospels, written between 70 and 100 C.E., are also pre-schism and represent communities within the diversity of first-century Judaism. In other words, there was not yet a Christianity separate from Judaism in the first century.

What has caused this change in perspective, from reading Paul's letters and the Gospels as written by Christians who separated from a defective Judaism, to interpreting the same literature as reflecting a distinctive first-century Jewish group among others? What has occurred that leads us to read these writings as part of an intra-Jewish controversy rather than Christianity's rejection of inferior Judaism?

Several developments in biblical studies have contributed to this shift in perspective. The ecumenical and interfaith context of biblical scholarship in the last few decades has led scholars to be more conscious of imposing confessional biases on the critical study of ancient texts. The study of biblical literature is no longer the exclusive domain of the church, interpreted to support particular doctrines or theories of origins. Secular institutions offer courses in biblical literature, and in nonreligious schools these courses are taught apart from the faith claims of any single religious group. As a result, the environment in which we study our Scriptures is conducive to a reexamination of the origins of Christianity and Judaism. A part of this new environment, too, is the heightened sensitivity to the history of Christianity's relationship with Judaism in the decades following the Holocaust, and an openness to see with new eyes.

The reconstruction of early Judaism apart from Christian bias has caused scholars to reconsider the context in which the Newer Testament literature was written. The evidence of primary sources indicates a wide range of expressions of Judaism, in Galilee and Judea as well as in the Diaspora. Recognizing the diversity of first-century Judaism challenges some of the Christian stereotypes of Judaism that affect how we understand the origin of Christianity and how we read the Newer Testament. For example, the traditional view of Christian origins supposes a normative (or orthodox, or rabbinic) Judaism from which Christianity separated. But if there was not a normative Judaism, then there was not a single defective expression of Judaism from which Christianity deviated. The idea of an early decisive departure from Judaism depends on the concept of a normative Judaism typically characterized by legalism, ethnic exclusivism, and the rejection of Jesus as Messiah. In the first century, those who claimed Jesus as Messiah and who later came to be called Christians belonged within the diversity of early Judaism. Both Christianity and Rabbinic Judaism were second-century developments emerging from the diversity of first-century Judaism.

Some scholars, observing the diversity of early Judaism, began to speak of "Judaisms."[1] This term, while capturing the reality of varieties of Judaism, begs the question: What defines Judaism? Certainly there were—and are—many different kinds of Judaism, but what are the boundaries that define early Judaism? What distinguishes someone or something as Jewish? What do both insiders and outsiders recognize as characteristics, customs, and beliefs that define Judaism? Drawing from primary sources, I propose three definers of early Judaism: the concept of a covenant relationship between the people Israel and their God, Torah observance, and the authority of Israel's Scriptures. Within each of these categories, there is a wide range of perspectives and practices.

The Covenant and the Relationship between Insiders and Outsiders

The covenant relationship between the people of Israel and their God who chose them out of all the peoples of the earth is fundamental to Israel's identity. This distinguishes them from all other peoples, and this distinction continues to define Israel as a people without geographical borders in the Diaspora. The concept of a people formed by a covenant relationship with the one, true God raises questions about belonging, who belongs, and how one belongs. It raises questions about the relationship between those who belong and those who do not. The relationship between insiders and outsiders, including how an outsider becomes an insider, becomes more complex in the Diaspora of the Greco-Roman period as Jews live as a minority among non-Jews.

Contrary to popular Christian belief, separation from Gentiles did not define early Judaism. The literature indicates a wide range of views on the relationship between Jews and others. First Maccabees provides a good illustration for disparate views within Israel. The book tells the story of the successful Maccabean (also called Hasmonean) revolt against persecution by the Seleucid King Antiochus Epiphanes IV. This is the story of Hanukkah and as such celebrates resistance against religious persecution. But the author of

1 Maccabees describes a civil controversy within Israel in the events leading up to Antiochus Epiphanes's intrusion into the political and cultural affairs in Judah:

> In those days certain renegades came out from Israel and misled many, saying, "Let us go and make a covenant with the Gentiles around us, for since we separated from them many disasters have come upon us." This proposal pleased them, and some of the people eagerly went to the king, who authorized them to observe the ordinances of the Gentiles. So they built a gymnasium in Jerusalem, according to Gentile custom, and removed the marks of circumcision, and abandoned the holy covenant. (1 Macc. 1:11-13)

The author's point of view favors those within Israel who resisted interaction with their non-Jewish neighbors and avoided accommodation to Greek culture. Clearly, though, there were Jews who welcomed interaction with their Gentile neighbors and did not oppose some of the benefits of Greek culture. What constituted apostasy from the author's perspective quite likely may have been regarded as a progressive reinterpretation of the covenant on the part of others. In Judea as well as in the Diaspora, Jews differed concerning the degree of interaction with the dominant culture.

The author of *Jubilees* advocates strict boundaries between those who belong to Israel and outsiders. Association with Gentiles poses a threat: "For they will forget all my commandments that I give them and copy the Gentiles, their uncleanness and their shame, and worship their gods; and these will prove a stumbling-block to them, a source of distress and misery, and a snare" (Prologue, v. 9).[2] Throughout *Jubilees*, the writer describes the Gentiles as idolaters, unclean, and sinful. The Dead Sea Scrolls witness to a sectarian community, separated not only from Gentiles but from other Jews, too. The Gospel of Matthew also reveals some negative images of Gentiles. In Matt. 5:46-47, Jesus, according to Matthew, says, "For if you love those who love you, what reward do you have? Do not even the tax collectors do the same? And if you greet only your brothers and sisters, what more are you doing than others? Do not even the Gentiles do the same?" And in 6:7, "When you are praying, do not heap up empty phrases as the Gentiles do; for they think that they will be heard because of their many words. Do not be like them . . ." The behavior of non-Jews is hardly admirable, and it functions here as a contrast to what is expected of Jews, including believing, or "christian" Jews. (I intentionally do not capitalize *christian* because I do not think that it was a proper noun in the first century. First-century "believers" later became known as "Christians," but when we use the familiar proper noun *Christian* in this context we tend to read later distinctions between Christianity and Judaism into the Gospels.)

Toward the other end of the spectrum, the first-century Jewish historian Josephus was influenced by Hellenistic culture and in his *Jewish Antiquities* (*Ant.*) presents the history of Israel in a way designed to appeal to other more Hellenized Jews and perhaps to non-Jews as well. For example, he describes the biblical heroes according to Hellenistic virtues. He tells of a meeting between Abraham and several learned Egyptians, and says of Abraham: "Thus gaining their admiration at these meetings as a man of extreme sagacity, gifted not only with high intelligence but with power to convince his hearers on any subject which he undertook to teach, he introduced them to arithmetic and transmitted to them the laws of astronomy" (*Ant.* 1:167–168).[3] According to Josephus, Moses delivers a lengthy speech modeled after the rubrics of Hellenistic historiography just before crossing the Red Sea, with the Egyptians in pursuit (*Ant.* 2:329–333). After the successful crossing of the Red Sea, Josephus tells us that Moses composed in hexameter verse a song to God (*Ant.* 2:346)! Josephus claims the Bible as his source, but he uses his source creatively, adapting it to accommodate the values of the dominant culture.

Philo, a Jewish philosopher from Alexandria writing in the mid-first century C.E., describes Judaism in terms comprehensible within the dominant culture. He likens the Law of Moses to law common to all societies. Philo defends the place of the proselyte in Israel and insists that one who converts to Judaism should have equal status within Israel with the one who belongs by virtue of birth.[4] One deduces from Philo's defense that the proselyte was accorded secondary status by some.

Was Judaism a proselytizing religion? The answer to that question depends on how one defines proselytism. If one views proselytism in terms of missionary activity with intention to convert others, then Judaism does not fit that model, familiar in Christianity. The Gospel of Matthew does tell us that the Pharisees actively sought out proselytes, but we do not know that they were non-Jews. In fact, that seems unlikely.[5] But if proselytism means more generally presenting one's religion, or way of life, in a way attractive to outsiders, and welcoming others into the community, then Jews did proselytize.

Whether or not we define Judaism as a proselytizing religion, the literary and material evidence shows that Judaism was well known and attractive to others. Latin satirists show disdain for Judaism and its strange customs, but they also indicate that some resentment toward Judaism is due in part to its attractiveness among some in the upper classes.[6] In Judea and Galilee as well as in the Diaspora, Gentiles related to Judaism in a wide range of ways, from admiration to full conversion.[7] According to the Acts of the Apostles, "god-fearers" in the synagogue, along with Israelites and proselytes, appear to be Gentiles who affiliate with Judaism—with the exception of circumcision.[8]

To summarize, a boundary defining Judaism is the covenant relationship with the God of Israel. This raises questions with respect to who belongs and how, the relationship between insiders and outsiders, and how others cross the boundary and become insiders. Jews exhibited a wide range of beliefs and practices concerning interaction with non-Jews, from strict avoidance to displaying hospitality and accommodation to the dominant culture. The common Christian view that Judaism was, and is, exclusively ethnocentric, that Jews uniformly avoided interaction with unclean Gentiles, and that non-Jews universally regarded Judaism with suspicion and contempt is historically inaccurate. Grasping the diversity of early Judaism in its interaction with others requires a more accurate construction of the history of Christian origins, and this will affect how we read the Newer Testament literature.

Torah Observance

Jews and Gentiles alike recognized Torah observance, or the Law of Moses, as a mark of Jewish identity. Circumcision was the rite of initiation into the covenant for males and the epitome of Torah observance. Circumcision so distinguished Jews from others that "circumcised" was a synonym for Jews. The Apostle Paul, for example, speaks of "the circumcised" and "the uncircumcised" (Gal. 2:7-9). Sabbath observance, the rest from work and the other daily activities on the seventh day, also separated Jews from others. And dietary laws, especially abstinence from eating pork, were well-known customs of Judaism. Within each one of these three categories of Torah observance, however, was a variety of practices among Jews.

I prefer the term "Torah observance" rather than "the Law." "Torah" means "instruction" or "way of life," and it is a matter of religious observance more than obedience to the Law. In Christian tradition there exists the misconception that the Law of Moses was an imposed burden rather than customs gladly observed as a matter of piety and identity. Psalm 119 provides a wonderful corrective to this misunderstanding, which persists in the interpretation of the Scriptures and the history of Christian definition over against Judaism.

Torah observance provided both common ground and ground for argument and debate among Jews. There was no central authority or institution that determined observance and made it binding on all Jews. There were, though, recognized teachers and sages who developed principles of interpretation. According to tradition, the School of Hillel and the School of Shammai represented two approaches to interpreting Torah observance, the former more lenient, the latter more stringent. What was customary varied from place to place and even within communities.

Circumcision

Even though circumcision was virtually synonymous with Jewish identity, nevertheless the question did emerge with respect to the circumcision of adult males who wished to convert to Judaism.[9] Josephus tells the story of Izates, king of Adiebene, who was attracted to Judaism and decided to convert. He intended to be circumcised, but his mother Helena, who admired Judaism, tried to persuade him against it, fearing that his subjects would not tolerate the rule of an adherent to a foreign religion. Izates consulted with a Jewish authority that agreed with Helena and opined that he could be a fully devoted adherent to Judaism without circumcision, considering the circumstances. But another Jewish authority that had a reputation for strict interpretation persuaded Izates that the Law of Moses required circumcision. Izates was circumcised immediately (*Ant.* 20:34-48).

To be sure, Josephus's story confirms the necessity of circumcision for an adult male proselyte, but it also presents two reasoned arguments from Jewish authorities on the question. I conclude from Josephus's narrative in *Jewish Antiquities* that the circumcision of adult males was not merely a hypothetical question among Jews. It stands to reason that, particularly where Jews lived as a minority among non-Jews and interacted with them, and as Judaism became more accessible to outsiders, the circumcision of adult males desiring to convert would generate debate. That the apostles of the Jesus movement, notably Paul, advocated circumcision-free membership in Israel did not place them outside the boundaries of Judaism.

Sabbath Observance

According to the first creation story in Genesis, "God blessed the seventh day and hallowed it, because on it God rested from all the work that he had done in creation" (Gen. 2:3). Written at the time of the Babylonian exile in the sixth century B.C.E., this narrative shows that Israel perceived Sabbath observance as woven into the fabric of creation from the very beginning. As God rested from God's creating, so Israel observes the seventh day as holy, set apart from the ordinary days of the week. The commandment to remember the Sabbath day and keep it holy (Exod. 20:8) cites the creation story as its rationale. From this commandment emerge several questions about observance. What is work? How does one protect the sanctity of the Sabbath? What separates the sacred from the ordinary? Under what circumstances is Sabbath observance suspended? The commandment generated a myriad of legal debates concerning these questions about the boundaries of Sabbath observance over the generations.

Needless to say, there is great diversity in the literature with respect to defining the boundaries of Sabbath observance. The *Mishnah*, the earliest recorded codification of rabbinic legal arguments, was redacted early in the third century C.E. It shows that the Sabbath was central to rabbinic thought, and that rabbinic authorities differed on definitions of keeping the Sabbath.[10] Sometimes a debate over a question declares a winner, by saying that the *halacha* is according to Rabbi so-and-so.[11] In other cases there is no tidy conclusion; two different perspectives stand without a ruling on correct observance. One gathers that the meaning is in the discussion of sacred matters more than offering a final judgment on customs. We must exercise caution in projecting later debates about Sabbath observance back into the early first century c.e., given that customs were transmitted orally. It is safe to say, however, that the differing opinions of the later rabbis were not more diverse than observance in the first century before the written compilation.

The Sabbath controversies in the Synoptic Gospels provide some insights into questions and customs of keeping the Sabbath when we read them within the context of Judaism rather than Jesus versus the Pharisees or Christians versus Jews.[12] Behind these controversies lie questions about what constitutes work, when customary observances may be suspended, and who has authority to define observance. In Christian interpretation, we often assume a rigid legalism in first-century Judaism that valued the Law over human need, and this was simply not the case. We will look more closely at these controversies in chapter 3, on the Pharisees and the Law.

Dietary Observances

Dietary observances originate in Leviticus, most notably the prohibition against eating pork and shellfish (Leviticus 11) and prescriptions concerning the slaughter and preparation of animals for consumption (Leviticus 17). These customs distinguished Jews from others; they were well known to Gentiles and sometimes were the source of ridicule.[13] In practice there were likely Jews who were stricter in "keeping kosher" than others, not unlike today. In the literature of the Greco-Roman period, however, the dietary customs most often at issue are related to eating the food and drinking the wine of Gentiles.

Jews exhibited varying degrees of interaction with Gentiles, as we noted above, from strict avoidance to welcoming interaction and accommodating behavior to the dominant culture. There are many instances in which Jews who interrelated with non-Jews nevertheless avoided the food and wine of Gentiles. According to the book of Esther, when Esther becomes queen she herself prepares the banquet for King Ahasuerus and Haman (chap. 5), and the apocryphal *Additions to Esther* assert that Esther did not eat at Haman's table nor eat or drink at the king's feast (14:17). Judith brings her own food and dishes when she goes to meet Holofernes (10:5), and when Holofernes invites her to join him for food and drink she refuses:

"I cannot partake of them, or it will be an offense; but I will have enough with the things I have brought with me" (Jdt. 12:1-3). Daniel refuses to eat the food and drink the wine offered at King Nebuchadnezzar's palace and requests only vegetables and water (Dan. 1:5, 8-16). The *Letter of Aristeas*, which narrates the legend about the translation of the Hebrew Scriptures into Greek, notes that the food at the king's banquet was prepared according to the customs of the Jewish translators (182–86).[14]

These are a few examples indicating that Jews who interacted with Gentiles and ate with them nevertheless refrained from eating their food or drinking their wine. The most likely reason for this was the suspicion, real or imagined, that the food and wine of Gentiles were associated in some way with idols and idol worship prior to its use for general consumption. We get some insight into this matter in Paul's first letter to the Corinthians in a discussion about whether it is acceptable to eat food that has been offered to idols (chap. 8). According to Talmudic scholar Gary Porton, the *Mishnah* and its companion, *Tosefta*, exhibit an obsession with the connection between Gentiles' wine and idols that he claims is quite unrealistic.[15]

Aversion to idolatry has a history as long as Israel's memory, so it is not surprising to read that Jews were careful, even obsessively so, about avoiding food and wine that may have had contact with idols. The instances mentioned above do not give the reason for abstaining from Gentiles' food, but that is not surprising either, in that the association between non-Jews and idolatry coupled with the repugnance of idols was a part of the ethos of Israel and was undoubtedly obvious to the reader.

In Christian tradition there is a tendency to conflate the avoidance of the food and wine of Gentiles with the avoidance of eating with Gentiles or with Gentiles themselves. Clearly, such avoidance was not the case. Some Jews did indeed refrain from any contact with non-Jews. Some did not sit at table with Gentiles. In Galatians, Paul rebukes Cephas for first eating with Gentiles and then refusing to eat with them, thus indicating some differences on matters of observance among the leadership of the believers in the mid-first century.[16] The literature of the period shows many instances of Jews eating with Gentiles, but the writers frequently make a point of telling us that these Jews did not eat the food or drink the wine offered by their Gentile hosts.

To summarize, Torah observance was a matter of Jewish identity, known to insiders and outsiders, and Jews were serious about defining how to live according to the traditions of the Law of Moses. Observance was a matter for debate and discussion. Since there was no central authority that determined universal customs, there was great diversity with respect to observances, including keeping the Sabbath, the dietary laws, and even circumcision, the rite of initiation, as it applied to adult male converts.

The Authority of Scripture

Israel had already by the beginning of the Common Era a long history of looking to its ancient sacred writings to inform its faith, customs, and identity. The Torah (Pentateuch) was the first collection of writings regarded as authoritative, then the prophetic works, followed by the recognition of "other writings." According to the Prologue of Ben Sira (also known as Ecclesiasticus or Sirach), written in the early part of the second century B.C.E., the Scriptures included the Law and the Prophets and "the other books of our ancestors." In the first century C.E., Josephus assumes writings beyond the Law and the Prophets. The writer of Luke-Acts includes the Psalms with the Law and the Prophets (Luke 24:44) and uses the Psalms extensively as scriptural support.

The account of Israel's gathering at the Water Gate in Nehemiah offers evidence within the Scriptures themselves of the authority of the Law of Moses (also called Torah, or Pentateuch). According to this narrative, Ezra reads from the book of the Law of Moses from an elevated platform, surrounded by a representative group of thirteen named individuals, in the presence of the whole assembly. When he opens the book the people all stand and respond to a blessing, saying "Amen, Amen," lifting their hands and bowing their heads and worshiping the Lord. A group of Levites help the people understand the Law, offering interpretation and giving the sense of the reading so the people understand.[17] We see here the reading of older texts in the context of a liturgical setting and *interpreting* them so that they have meaning in the present.

In the Second Temple period, as today, communities that claimed the authority of the Scriptures appealed to these ancient writings in order to define Judaism in their own time and place. The Scriptures represent one of the unifying boundaries of Judaism, but there was a wide diversity of methods of interpretation and, of course, different understandings of the meaning of these ancient texts.

The translation of the Scriptures from Hebrew into the vernacular languages is one kind of interpretation. The translation of the Scriptures into Greek, called the Septuagint, was completed in the third century B.C.E. as Greek became the first language of many Jews living in the Diaspora. This translation also made the ancient writings of the Jews accessible to non-Jews, and these writings were known and respected among educated Gentiles. The *Targumim* paraphrased the writings in Aramaic and provided a kind of running commentary on the Hebrew texts as they were read in liturgical settings.

Retelling the biblical narratives was another method of interpretation. We see this method within the Scriptures in Chronicles, which is the last book in the *Tanak*.[18] The narrative closely follows the books of Samuel and Kings but offers a distinctive theological perspective through the addition of speeches and omissions. Josephus uses the biblical narratives as a primary source for *Jewish Antiquities* but, as we noted earlier, presents the heroes of Israel in accordance with the values of Hellenistic culture. *Jubilees* also retells the narratives of antiquity to claim the authority of the Scriptures for its distinctive calendar.

Philo employs allegory; so does the Apostle Paul. For example, Paul offers an allegorical interpretation of Sarah and Hagar to defend his argument for including non-Jews in the covenant on the basis of faith in Jesus Christ without observing the Law of Moses (Galatians 4). The Qumran community used a promise-fulfillment method of interpretation called *pesher* to support their view of the Teacher of Righteousness. This method is similar to the method of interpretation we see often used in the Gospels to validate beliefs about Jesus, a method most apparent in the first two chapters of Matthew where we see the repetition of the fulfillment of the prophets in the narratives of Jesus' birth and his early childhood in Egypt.

The selection of texts to read is in itself an interpretive choice. In the period of formative Judaism following the destruction of the Temple in 70 C.E., different groups selected different parts of Scripture to define Judaism. The early rabbinic movement relied primarily on Leviticus, Exodus, and Deuteronomy to establish the identity of Israel. They developed principles of exegesis they applied systematically to these biblical books containing the origins of Torah observance.[19] Those who believed in Jesus Messiah, on the other hand, looked primarily to the prophets to establish scriptural support for their understanding of the formation of Judaism and covenant relationship with the God of Israel.

There existed wide diversity in the ways Jews in the Second Temple period interpreted their ancient sacred texts, but they held in common a reverence for the ancient writings in defining the relationship between the people Israel and their God. They appealed to these Scriptures to authenticate their perspectives on matters of observance, associations with outsiders, and their understanding of the God who had made a covenant with them. The acknowledged authority of the Scriptures is a distinctive unifying characteristic of Judaism, distinguishing Jews from others; Jews differed among themselves in their methods of exegesis and interpretations.

The Gospels *Were* Jewish Literature

Drawing from primary sources, I have identified three attendant boundaries that defined early Judaism, namely, a covenant relationship, Torah observance, and the authority of Israel's Scriptures. Both Jews themselves and non-Jews recognized these three as characteristics of Jewish identity. Within these parameters, there was broad diversity in practice and attitudes. In the above representative selections from sources, I have emphasized evidence that challenges some typical Christian misconceptions about Judaism that influence how we read the Newer Testament. Along with the established Jewish literature, I have included references to Paul and the Gospels as I am convinced that they belong within the diversity of first-century Judaism.

My focus here is on the Gospels as Jewish literature. In the first place, many scholars have convincingly placed Paul within Judaism rather than as a Christian who has rejected his Jewish heritage. More importantly, this book is about Christian preaching and the problem of anti-Judaism. The Gospels, particularly the Synoptics, are primary sources for preaching. They are also primary sources for perpetuating anti-Jewish stereotypes. I propose to demonstrate that the Gospels belong within the context of early Judaism. When we better understand this context, I believe we will be better equipped to counter some of the misconceptions about Judaism and Christian origins that continue to surface in sermons.

The Gospels share the characteristics of Jewish identity in that they tell the continuing story of Israel's relationship with its God. They presuppose a covenant relationship and an interest in who belongs and how. The matter of Torah observance is also frequently an issue, and the authority of the Scriptures is assumed. The supposition of the authority of the Scriptures is the most obvious. Each of the Synoptic Gospels indicates at the beginning of the story that the author is invested in the ancient sacred writings of Israel.[20] The truth about what God is doing in and for Israel must be grounded in the Scriptures.

Mark, the earliest of the canonical Gospels, begins with a citation from Isaiah, and in doing so signals that he expects the audience (readers and/or hearers) to be persuaded by the "proof text" he puts forward for John the Baptist as the one who prepares the way for the coming Messiah. Indeed, the idea of a forerunner to the appearance of Israel's Messiah, God's anointed, supposes an understanding of Israel's history and future expectations about God's relations with God's people.

Matthew begins with a genealogy that includes, without any explanation, the names of four women besides Mary, none of them particularly prominent in the Scriptures. The author apparently assumes that the audience knows who these women are and will understand the purpose in inserting them into the genealogy. In the annunciation and birth narrative that follows in the first chapter, the obvious appeal to Scripture is in the citation of Isa. 7:14,[21] but there is also the allusion to a dreamer named Joseph, lending credibility to revelation in dreams. And, as mentioned above, there are many references to the fulfillment of the prophets in the first two chapters of Matthew.

In Christian tradition, the Gospel of Luke has the reputation of Gentile authorship and audience and less dependence on the Scriptures of Israel. A careful read of Luke-Acts, however, indicates that this Gospel is grounded in the Scriptures in both obvious and more subtle ways. Immediately following the elegantly constructed introduction (vv. 1-4), the author makes an abrupt transition, mimicking biblical language (in Greek translation), hinting to the audience to read or hear the narrative as a continuation of Israel's history recounted in the Scriptures. One can hear this even in the English translation: "In the days of King Herod of Judea, there was a priest named Zechariah . . ." (v. 5). And to ears familiar with the stories of the patriarchs and matriarchs, the situation of Elizabeth and Zechariah echoes that of Abraham and Sarah: "Both of them were righteous before God, living blamelessly according to all the commandments and regulations of the Lord. But they had no children, because Elizabeth was barren, and both were getting on in years" (vv. 6-7). The song of Mary (vv. 46-55) parallels the song of Hannah (1 Sam. 2:1-10) and includes many allusions to the Psalms. There are many allusions and references to the Scriptures in the prologue (chapters 1–2), indicating that the writer knows these writings thoroughly, and supposes as well that the audience knows them and shares his regard for them.

The Gospels are incomprehensible apart from the Hebrew Scriptures. It would require a book much longer than this to cover adequately this dependence in even one Gospel. For purposes of illustration, I have selected examples from the first chapter of each Synoptic Gospel, because it is in the beginning of a work that a writer presents clues to the audience as to how to read or hear what follows, and what is the author's purpose, suppositions, worldview, commitments, and expectations with respect to the audience's knowledge and social and religious location. Obviously the Gospel writers take for granted the authority of Israel's Scriptures in making the case for Jesus' identity as God's Messiah.

In Luke 10:25-28, there is a brief exchange between a lawyer and Jesus that illustrates well the place of the Scriptures in early Judaism. The lawyer asks Jesus what he must do to inherit eternal life. Jesus responds with two questions. The first: "What is written in the law?" And the second: "How do you read?"[22] The lawyer responds with a verse from Deuteronomy and a verse from Leviticus: "You shall love the Lord your God with all your heart, and with all your soul, and with all your strength, and with all your mind [Deut. 6:5], and your neighbor has yourself [Lev. 19:18]." The lawyer tells Jesus what he reads in the Law, and then by putting two verses together, he interprets what he reads, drawing from the Scriptures to answer a current question of faith and practice. Jesus agrees with the lawyer's interpretation. Here in Luke, not unlike in Nehemiah, we see evidence of the authority of the Scriptures as the primary source for addressing religious matters, and we see also the supposition that what is read must be interpreted. The Gospel writers take for granted the world of diverse and competing scriptural interpretation in first-century Judaism.

With respect to Torah observance, Mark gives the least attention of the three Synoptics to this defining characteristic of early Judaism. The author includes two Sabbath controversies (2:23—3:6) pitting Jesus against the Pharisees. In the first, Jesus quotes Scripture to defend the disciples' plucking grain on the Sabbath. The final statement suggests that what is at stake is who has the authority to determine what is lawful on the Sabbath: "The Son of Man is lord even of the sabbath" (v. 28). The second involves healing on the Sabbath and portrays Jesus as the humanitarian willing to heal the man with the withered hand, in opposition to the Pharisees. Several chapters later, Mark's Jesus criticizes the Pharisees as hypocrites for observing human tradition while rejecting God's commandments (7:1-13). Christians tend to read these controversies as historically reliable descriptions of the Pharisees and the rejection of the Law. I suggest that they represent part of the debate over Jewish definition among different groups, and the polemic against the Pharisees is what one would expect from the Jesus movement seeking to establish its claims as the legitimate heir of the promises of God to Israel.

Matthew contains the strongest polemic against the Pharisees and Torah observance. The litany in chapter 23 against "scribes and Pharisees, hypocrites" (v. 13) is scathing. But notice how this chapter begins: "The scribes and Pharisees sit on Moses' seat; therefore, do whatever they teach you and follow it" (v. 2). In other words, Matthew's Jesus acknowledges the authority of the scribes and Pharisees to interpret the Law of Moses and advises the disciples to follow what they teach (but, he continues, not what they do!). Earlier, Matthew holds the Pharisees up as models of righteousness: "For I tell you, unless your righteousness *exceeds* that of the scribes and Pharisees you will never enter the kingdom of heaven" (5:20; emphasis mine). Righteousness, in Matthew, frequently implies observance, and the connection here with the Pharisees implies that meaning. The polemic against the Pharisees and controversies over Torah observance in this Gospel indicate a passionate engagement concerning the Law on the part of the writer of Matthew, and this suggests an intra-Jewish controversy over who best represents authentic Judaism in the decades following the destruction of the Temple in 70 C.E.[23]

The Gospel of Luke confirms the importance of Torah observance in its prologue and thereby suggests to the reader of Luke-Acts that this will be an important part of the continuing story of Israel. We learn that Zechariah and Elizabeth "were righteous," that is, they lived "blamelessly according to all the commandments and regulations of the Lord" (v. 6). Both John and Jesus are circumcised on the eighth day (1:59; 2:21). According to Luke, Jesus' parents are meticulous in observing the Law following his birth. Observance of the Law is mentioned specifically five times (2:22, 23, 24, 27, 39) and alluded to in describing Simeon as "righteous and devout" and Anna as devoted to three prominent aspects of observance—worship, fasting, and prayer (vv. 25 and 37, respectively). Beyond the prologue, Luke includes two Sabbath narratives in addition to a redacted version of the two in Mark and Matthew. Luke's redaction of the two in Mark softens the polemic and indicates an intra-Pharisaic debate (6:1-11). The two that are unique (13:10-17; 14:1-6) to Luke are set at a Sabbath meal with Pharisees, and thus also intimates intra-Pharisaic debate.

Luke presents Jesus within the Law, differing with the Pharisees on interpretation and claiming authority as an interpreter of the Law. And in Acts, the sequel to Luke, Paul is a meticulously observant Pharisee.[24] According to Acts, some Pharisees are believers (15:5); others defend the believers (5:34-39; 23:9). There is no general condemnation of the Pharisees, the recognized interpreters of the Law, in Luke-Acts, nor is there a rejection of the importance of Torah observance. The Gentile mission in Acts does not require circumcision of adult male converts, but other aspects of observance continue as marks of identity for followers of the Way.[25]

The Synoptic Gospels and Acts, written between 70–100 C.E., show that the matter of Torah observance in the nascent "christian" communities was far from settled. The question of identity, how believers were like and not like other Jews, was a live issue. The sharp polemic against the Pharisees in Matthew distinguishes the Matthean community from them in terms of motives and sincerity in observance. Luke-Acts in the prologue affirms Torah observance in the presentation of key figures. Though less prominent, there are a few legal controversies with the Pharisees in Mark. Attention to

Torah observance places the Gospels within the context of the process of Jewish self-definition in the latter part of the first century.

The destruction of the Temple in 70 C.E. caused a crisis of faith and identity in Judaism. The Temple in Jerusalem was a unifying symbol and focus for Jews in the Greco-Roman period. In its absence, questions about God, the covenant relationship, and the identity of Israel took on urgency. Has God abandoned Israel? Where now is God active in the affairs of Israel and the world? Which Jews rightfully claim to be heirs of the promises of God to Israel? Who is faithful to the covenant relationship with God? Who are we, now that God's dwelling place and holy city is destroyed? These were not abstract or theoretical questions. The faith and future of Israel were at stake. In the wake of devastation following the war against Rome, Jews answered these defining questions differently.

These questions are central to the Synoptic Gospels. According to the Gospels (and Paul, too, of course), one belonged to faithful Israel by virtue of faith in Jesus, God's Messiah. Gentiles were included by acknowledging Jesus as the Messiah of the God of Israel. As we have shown above, the Gospels do not agree with Paul's assertion that Gentiles need not observe the Law of Moses.[26] The Gospels do assert that "Jesus is the answer," but it matters what the questions are. The questions emerged within the context of Judaism and the process of identity formation at the end of the first century. The Gospels' response to these questions does not place them outside of Judaism, but rather within the sphere of discussion and debate and deliberation with other Jews regarding the future of Israel.

Christian readers tend to miss the centrality of the faith and identity questions in the Gospels because, in the first place, they are implied rather than stated. They were presupposed as part of the shared worldview of author and audience. But also, we read the Gospels in light of our own experience, that is, as Christian writings, supposing the separation of Christianity from Judaism and projecting that reality back into the first century. And we frequently read later Christian doctrine into the Gospels. We typically read the Gospels from a *christocentric* perspective, assuming that the primary purpose is to tell the story of Jesus Christ, or even confirming the divinity of Jesus.

When we read from a *theocentric* perspective, we hear the story of Jesus in relationship to the story of the God of Israel. God is the unseen "main character" in the story. Jesus' significance is in his role as God's Messiah, that is, the anointed one, prophet, and son. In other words, the Gospels do not think of Jesus as God.[27] Claims about Jesus in effect answer unspoken questions about what God is doing in and for Israel.

For example, when I ask students about the main point of the citation of Isa. 7:14 in Matt. 1:23, most answer quite quickly that it proves the virgin birth and the divinity of Jesus. I suggest that the new name given to Jesus may be just as important, if not more so. There is a shift in pronoun in Matthew's version of the quote from Isaiah. According to Isaiah, the mother names her child Immanuel. According to Matthew, ". . . they shall name him Immanuel." With that subtle change, it is as if the narrator tells us, "His parents named him Jesus, but you all might call him Immanuel, which means 'God is with us'; look here, to this child, to the life and teachings of Jesus, and you will see God with us, in the midst of Israel." The question was not, in the first place, "Who is Jesus?" The implied questions were about Israel's God. Has God abandoned Israel? Is God with us or not? We will read differently when we consider these questions behind the Gospel narratives.

The last third of the first century was a critical formative period for the identity and future of Judaism. By the middle of the next century a schism occurred between two surviving groups claiming to be heirs of the promises of God to Israel, and rabbinic Judaism and Christianity developed along different paths. The historical context for the Gospels, though, is that formative period within Judaism during which Jews sought to define the boundaries of Israel in new ways in light of the destruction of the Temple. Given what was at stake, we should not be surprised by the passion and polemic in the Jewish literature of this period. The controversies and polemic we read in the Gospels are indicative of passionate engagement in the questions of belonging and identity that would determine the future of Judaism.

Summary

The Gospels belong within the context of the diversity of early Judaism. They represent constituents of the wide variety of expressions of Judaism in the first century who shared with other Jews the commitment to the covenant relationship with the God of Israel, Torah observance as a mark of identity, and the authority of the Scriptures. The criticisms of *other* Jewish groups were part of an intra-Jewish debate over the identity and future of Israel. I advise readers to make a distinction between the long history of anti-Jewish interpretation and the Gospels themselves. It is anachronistic to read them as an interreligious controversy, setting Christianity in opposition to Judaism. Preachers who bear in mind the diversity of early Judaism and the place of the Gospels within that context will be less likely to rely on anti-Jewish stereotypes in sermons.

2

Supersessionism

SUPERSESSIONISM is the belief that Christianity replaced Judaism as heir of the promises of God to Israel. It is the conventional account of the history and theology of Christian origins. A long-standing interpretation of the Scriptures supports this version of Christian history and theology. Clearly there is no place for Judaism in this account of the Christian story in which Christianity supersedes the old covenant of God with Israel, becoming the "new Israel" constituted by faith in Jesus Christ.

The most overt expressions of supersessionism include the following: the Jews rejected Jesus; the Old Testament shows the Jews as disobedient and unrepentant; Judaism at the time of Jesus knew only a transcendent, remote God; Judaism in the first century was defined by hypocritical legalism and obsession with ritual apart from any spiritual motives, the Pharisees serving as primary example; the Old Testament describes a God of wrath, in contrast to the God of love in the New Testament. Because of their faithlessness and obduracy therefore, God rightly rejected the Jews in favor of the predominantly Gentile Church.

I suspect that most readers would reject these blatant statements of supersessionism. Several denominations have taken positions formally rejecting it, along with other forms of anti-Judaism. Robert Jenson asserts that few theologians are willing to be called supersessionists. He suggests a few reasons for this. One is guilt for the centuries of anti-Jewish polemics that shaped the culture that made anti-Semitism possible. Another is that we see ever more clearly how deeply indebted Christianity is to Judaism, and that "the church is indeed grafted on to someone else's tree."[1] Further, in an era of pluralism and awareness of global connectedness, many Christians are interested in other religions and actively seek understanding and knowledge of them. Liberal Christianity typically affirms the integrity of other expressions of faith, honoring God's freedom of self-revelation outside Christianity. We do not claim that Christians hold an exclusive claim to truth about God. There exists, therefore, an openness to seeing the Jewishness of our roots, some of which continue in our patterns of liturgy and prayer.

Changes in terminology indicate liberal Christianity's official rejection of supersessionism. For instance, late Judaism has become early Judaism! Until the latter part of the last century, scholars typically referred to Judaism in the century before and after the birth of Jesus as late Judaism. If that was late Judaism, what do we call Judaism today? The term "late Judaism" represents a not-so-subtle denial of the continuation of Judaism beyond the beginning of Christianity. The abbreviations B.C.E. (Before the Common Era) and C.E. (Common Era) are now the preferred terms in ecumenical and secular conversations for the confessionally biased B.C. and A.D. The terms used with increasing frequency for the parts of the Christian Bible reflect sensitivity to Christianity's relationship with Judaism: Older and Newer Testaments, First and Second Testaments, Hebrew Bible rather than Old Testament.

We have not, however, effectively reconstructed the conventional story of our history, nor the theology of origins, nor the traditional interpretations of our Scriptures in keeping with our rejection of the overt expressions of supersessionism. Preachers who renounce supersessionism continue to rely on a supersessionist history of Christian origins. Many who reject anti-Judaism nevertheless espouse the view that Christianity replaced a defective Judaism by interpreting biblical texts to display the superior qualities of Jesus and the early churches at the expense of inferior, unenlightened Jews.

Defining Christianity over against Judaism

"Does Christianity *have* to identify itself as that which is over and against Judaism?"[2] A literal reading of the Newer Testament, in particular, seems to confirm a Christianity defined over and against Judaism. It is not surprising, therefore, that we read the familiar stories of Jesus in light of a well-rehearsed story line. And, as we observed above, emphasizing the contrast between Jesus and his opponents in the story works well in homiletics to accentuate the point of a sermon. But it is not inevitable that Christianity define itself in sharp contrast to Judaism.

As we observed in the preceding chapter, the history of Christian and Jewish origins is much more complex than the traditional Christian (and Jewish) account allows. The primary sources indicate a wide diversity in first-century Judaism, and the early messianist movement was a part of that diversity of early Judaism. Christianity did not have an identity separate from Judaism until well into the second century.[3] So, on historical grounds, not only is it unnecessary to identify Christianity over and against Judaism, it is anachronistic to read this schism into the canonical Gospels or to attribute to Jesus opposition to Judaism. With respect to Jesus, we cannot maintain simultaneously that he was a faithfully observant Jew and that he stood in opposition to a defective Judaism. Criticisms on the part of Jesus and the later Gospel communities belong to intra-Jewish controversies, not to a Christian judgment of flaws in Judaism.

In the second and third centuries, as Judaism and Christianity took separate paths, there is indeed a strain of *adversus Iudaeos* in Christian literature. But let us place these writings in context, too. It is important to remember that the heavier burden of self-definition fell upon Christianity to establish the continuity of its history within Judaism while at the same time distinguishing itself from Jews who claimed the same Scriptures and religious symbols. The polemic against Judaism served the needs of Christian self-definition and identity formation in its separation from Judaism. This polemic evidences little real contact with Jews and often reveals a misunderstanding of Jewish customs.[4] In the case of John Chrysostom's virulent attacks on Judaism (c. 400), they were a reaction to Christians in his charge who were Judaizers; they were observing some Jewish customs, such as attending Sabbath services. Judaism represented a threat because of its attraction to some Christians who knew the histories and Scriptures held in common and did not fully grasp the distinct identities.[5] Unfortunately, in the post-Constantine world when Christianity became the religion of the Empire, the *adversus Iudaeos* theme dominated the Christian story of origins, though it no longer served its earlier function of defining the identity of a minority. In the hands of a dominant majority, this polemic against Judaism served to marginalize, demonize, and oppress Jews, now a minority in the Western world. In Christianity's early formation, the *adversus Iudaeos* argument, though hardly admirable, is understandable and, absent political power, did little damage. That it continued has led to a tragic history; that it continues after the Shoah is reprehensible.

Why does this supersessionist construction of Christian history continue, even among those who reject supersessionism, who are committed to mending relationships between Jews and Christians? A problem for Christians is that, in our myth of origins, history and theology and biblical interpretation are inexorably bound together. According to the traditional account of history, Jesus criticized the Judaism of his day, and the messianist movement that followed spread quickly beyond Judaism where it was received by Gentiles. The letters of Paul, the Gospels, and the Acts of the Apostles purportedly tell this history. Christian theology provides the interpretation: the Christian gospel proclaimed God's love known in Jesus Christ, contrasted with a transcendent, unapproachable God; Christianity grasped God's grace in contrast to the burden of earning salvation by obeying the Law (a traditional reading of Paul's letters); Christianity's universalism provided a corrective to Judaism's ethnic exclusivism; Christians followed Jesus in rejecting Judaism's focus on empty ritual in favor of rightly motivated deeds. And, of course, a literal reading of the Scriptures provides the authoritative historical and theological grounding for the prevailing story of Christian beginnings. Christian investment in this account is historical, theological, and biblical.

But clearly, it is not necessary to proclaim the gospel of Jesus Christ at the expense of Judaism. The revelation of God's love in Jesus Christ does not depend on a supposed emphasis on God's wrath or judgment, or the inadequate grasp of God's love in Judaism. The immanence of God embodied in Christ does not require a Judaism that knew only transcendence. The proclamation of God's grace that Christians know through faith in Christ does not need the Law as a foil. Christianity's claim of offering salvation to all does not require the creation of an "other" that limits salvation to only some.

Christianity does not have to define itself over and against Judaism. In the first place, the conventional story of origins is not historically accurate. It depends on a construction of Judaism created by Christianity for its own purposes. Second, it relies on a superficial reading of Paul and the Gospels that does not take into account the context of a diverse first-century Judaism. And finally, Christian theology does not require a deficient Judaism for authentic proclamation. But the supersessionist story line is deeply imbedded in our imaginations, so we need to be intentional in learning a truer story of Christian origins, including how the traditional story line is constantly reinforced in the ways we read, interpret, and preach the Scriptures.

In this chapter, we will look first at the relationship between the Testaments and the ways the simple fact of an "Old Testament" and a "New Testament" in the Christian Bible contributes to supersessionism. Second, we will see how historical-Jesus studies have reinforced supersessionism by defining Jesus over and against the Judaism of his time. Finally, liberal theologies frequently depend upon a caricature of Judaism and thus endorse supersessionism among those of us most likely to be sensitive to the problem of anti-Judaism. In addition to raising awareness of how supersessionism continues in biblical interpretation and preaching, I will suggest strategies for countering it.

Relationship between the Testaments

The simple fact that the Christian Bible includes what is commonly called an Old Testament and a New Testament continues to reinforce the way we interpret and preach the Scriptures. In the second century, when Christianity claimed Israel's Scriptures as its own and designated them "Old Testament," the church created a dilemma that is still with us. What is the relationship between what Christians call the Old Testament and the New Testament? How are Christians to interpret the Scriptures that tell the story of Israel before the life of Jesus, history shared with Judaism? Ironically, the very fact that the early church retained the Scriptures of Jesus and of Paul and of the Gospel communities in its canon intensifies the *adversus Iudaeos* tradition.

The classic definition of the relationship between Old and New is that the New supersedes the Old. In the Old Testament, we encounter a God of wrath, replaced by the God of love in Jesus Christ. The

New Covenant defined by grace replaces the Old Covenant defined by the Law. The story of the Old Covenant is one of disobedience, continued in the Jews' willful rejection of Jesus, and consequently God's rejection of them. According to traditional interpretations, the Old Testament points to the New, predicts Jesus, and its prophecies find fulfillment in the New Testament.

Efforts to rename the Old Testament indicate an awareness of the supersessionism implicit in the division of our Bible into two distinct parts. But most of the commonly used labels are inadequate. Some actually deepen the wedge. The counterpart to "Hebrew Bible" or "Hebrew Scriptures" becomes "Christian Scriptures." But the "Hebrew Scriptures" are also Christian Scriptures, are they not? "Older" and "Newer" may be the most satisfactory labels, but these have not attained common usage. Perhaps most problematic is the continued use of "Testament," which still implies a covenant that is newer and better than the former one. But renaming the parts of the Christian Bible is only the beginning and not a solution to supersessionism. The development of interpretive methods must accompany a heightened awareness of the ways we subjugate the older Scriptures to the so-called greater truths revealed in the Newer Testament.

I doubt that the most overt forms of supersessionism occur often in sermons delivered by preachers educated in most mainline seminaries. Seminary Older Testament courses tend to dispel the most blatant supersessionist interpretations; indeed, they likely foster a deep appreciation for the faith of God's people and God's compassion and love and grace revealed in this literature. The most common expression of discontinuity between Testaments surfaces in preaching on Newer Testament texts that cite our Older Testament texts. The way we interpret these texts often reinforces the view that the New replaces the Old, though that is likely not the intent.

The most common example is the citation of prophecies that are said to be fulfilled in Jesus. The Gospel writers applied a promise-fulfillment method of interpretation; so the text says that something "fulfills what was written in the prophets." The lectionaries frequently pair "the promise" from the Older Testament with "the fulfillment" from the Newer Testament, implying a simple connection between an Older Testament text and the correct meaning the

Gospel assigns to it. Further, Christians may have an investment in the belief that the "proof texts" actually prove the claims we make about Jesus the Christ, about his birth, his role as the Suffering Servant, his identity as the Messiah, for example. When we take the first-century prophecy-fulfillment method literally, the effect is to remove a Newer Testament prophecy citation from the world of biblical interpretation and assign it a single, true, and obvious meaning. Even if the preacher is aware of the flaws in the literal reading, it requires intention and planning to take a sermon in a different direction.

A clear understanding of both prophecy and fulfillment provides a good exegetical foundation. In the first place, a prophet is an interpreter of the present, one who sees the world from God's perspective, who speaks a word of comfort or judgment, in relationship to the present and the near future. The prophetic word is the right word spoken at the right time, and it is meaningful in its own time. And it requires discernment on the part of God's people to determine who speaks the word of God. How does one know who speaks the truth about what God is doing in relationship to God's people? According to Deut. 18:21-22, one knows if a prophet speaks in the name of the Lord if what he prophesies happens. So, we must wait to see how things turn out! But the rubric set forth in Deuteronomy is not a very helpful guide in the present, when faithful people assess God's presence in the world differently.

Jeremiah 28 tells the story of Hananiah, a prophet who claims to speak for the Lord, who assures the people that God will not allow the destruction of Jerusalem. Jeremiah has a different vision of what God will do, prophesying a hard word to hear, that the people depend too much on the security of the Temple (26:1-6), and that it will be destroyed. The prophecies of Jeremiah are canonized because Jerusalem, including the Temple, was destroyed and the people taken into exile in the sixth century B.C.E., in Jeremiah's own lifetime. *In retrospect*, Jeremiah's prophecies became part of Israel's self-criticism, their disobedience a cause for the exile. I wonder, had I heard Jeremiah and Hananiah prophesy conflicting views of "Thus says the Lord," which one would have convinced me he discerned the truth about God. In the same vein, we might wonder how we would have responded to competing claims about God's word for Israel in the first century. A prophetic word must always be placed in the context in which it originated, and the various contexts in which it is reinterpreted, including the first century and the twenty-first century.

A more nuanced understanding of fulfillment will also benefit the homilist. The word translated "fulfill" has the meaning of "corresponds to," or "is analogous to," or "reminds one of."[6] For example, Jesus' suffering corresponds to the one of whom Isaiah speaks (Isaiah 53), who suffers for the sake of Israel. Herod's murder of the innocent children of Jerusalem (Matt. 2:16-18) reminds the author of the lost children for whom Rachel weeps (Jer. 31:15), and, I add, reminds us of the loss of innocent children in our own times. The betrayal of Jesus is analogous to an earlier event in Israel (John 13:18 and Ps. 41:9).[7]

Also, as we read our Scriptures in English translation, we remind ourselves that a translation involves interpretation. The Newer Testament writers read their Scriptures in translation, too. Sometimes the "fulfillment" of a prophecy depends on a Greek translation of the Hebrew text. This is the case in Matthew's citation of Isa. 7:14, for example. The Septuagint translates the Hebrew "young woman" as "virgin." That translation from Hebrew to Greek lends itself to Matthew's use. We remember, too, that when interpreting the Scriptures, prophecy and fulfillment work backwards, beginning with the convictions of the interpreters. The Newer Testament authors believed Jesus was God's Messiah, and they interpreted the Scriptures in light of faith. They began with their convictions about Jesus and looked to the Scriptures to support their understanding of what God was doing among them in their own times.

What might these insights about prophecy and fulfillment look like in a sermon? Excerpts from a homily I preached on the annunciation and birth of Jesus according to Matthew illustrate one approach to this familiar prophecy-fulfillment text. My suppositions about the interpretation of prophecy and fulfillment within contexts and informed by the convictions of the interpreter are implicit in the sermon. Also, a close reading of both Isaiah 7 and Matthew's citation of 7:14 shows that, according to Matthew, "they" name the child "Immanuel," not the child's mother, as Isaiah has it. I think the change was an intentional exegetical move on the part of the Gospel writer, as if to say, "They all will call him Immanuel." I also think this subtle move shifts the emphasis somewhat from a virgin birth to Jesus' identity as Immanuel, a name given to Jesus only here.

I began the sermon with the observation that the name the parents give the child is Jesus, not Immanuel:

All this took place to fulfill what the Lord had spoken by the prophet: and behold a virgin shall conceive and bear a son and they shall name him Immanuel. But, they didn't name him Immanuel. They named him Jesus. We know that and so does Matthew, because he says so, in the very next verse. "They called his name Jesus." So why, then, does Matthew quote from Isaiah a verse about a young woman bearing a child whom she named Immanuel? What does that have to do with Jesus, son of Mary and Joseph, born eight centuries later?

I identified the theme, "Immanuel, God with us," as the interpretive connection between Isaiah and Matthew, and also with us. The premise that "God with us" always requires discernment and interpretation is evident in what follows, as is the conviction that God is faithful:

It's the sign. The Lord will give you a sign, Isaiah says to doubting King Ahaz, a sign that God is faithful. In the midst of doubt and uncertainty, a sign that God is with us—call the sign Immanuel. The Gospel of Matthew shares a fundamental conviction with the prophet Isaiah, the conviction that God is faithful. Dependable. God keeps promises. Matthew sees the sign Immanuel, God with us, manifest in the person named Jesus. Immanuel, God with us, in the ordinary and unexpected. God is with us, in the darkness. Name the sign Immanuel.

It is still Advent. It is not yet light; the darkness fades; the light is near but not yet. It is still difficult to see, to discern the sign. And so I am thankful for those before me who could see, in the darkness of doubt, and say, in the ambiguous gray, Immanuel, God with us.

For the prophet Isaiah, who nagged a frightened king facing a political and theological crisis, the city of Jerusalem under siege, the only hope seemingly a foreign alliance and military action. Wait. Be patient. Trust God to be faithful to Israel. In the time it takes to conceive and bear and bring a child to the age of reason, the siege will be ended and God's holy city will be safe. Name the sign Immanuel. God is with us.

I'm thankful, too, for Ahaz, who exasperated God by stubbornly refusing to ask for a sign. Was it out of fear of rejection and disappointment? If you don't expect God to do anything or to be there, you can't be disappointed. If you don't ask for a sign, you can't be let down. It's comforting to hear that God is weary-resistant, persistent in giving signs of Immanuel, to those with discerning hearts, even stubborn ones.

I give thanks for Joseph the dreamer, who saw and heard in his dreams, while it was yet dark, what he could not understand in the wakeful hours of daylight. What is the just, the righteous thing to do? Don't be afraid, Joseph, to do what others may not perceive as righteous. Trust your dreams, Joseph, your intuition, what you perceive in the solitude of night. Immanuel, God is with you. The light will come.

It is still Advent, not yet light, but discerning hearts perceive Immanuel, where there is doubt, where death intrudes, knowing no Christmas truce. I am thankful for the prophetic ones who see and hear the signs before the rest of us, and point to the fulfillment of promise, of God with us. And I am thankful for those who share the routine, the daily-ness of my life—family and friends, colleagues and students, the people I worship with in this place—these sign for me in the ordinary and often unexpected ways, Immanuel, by giving and receiving love, in listening, encouraging, hoping, challenging, forgiving. God is with us.

It is still Advent, but soon, very soon, Christmas comes. Our light comes, to illumine the darkness, and we will gather again to see it, to hear it, to say it, Jesus, our Immanuel, the sign, God is with us.[8]

Preachers will develop their own methods of interpreting the classic prophecy-fulfillment texts, depending on the text, the season, and other variables that shape a sermon. The beginning point is the awareness of the way a literal prophecy-fulfillment scheme reinforces supersessionism and a resolve to explore alternatives.

Practices of First-Century Judaism

Another common reading of Newer Testament citations of Scripture that results in supersessionism is to assume that customs described in the Torah were still the practices of first-century Jews, as if nothing had changed in Judaism for several centuries. When we do so, we assert the superiority of Newer Testament understandings of the Older Testament as well as negate the continuing development of Judaism. The so-called "antitheses" in the fifth chapter of Matthew provide a good example. Jesus says, several times, "You have heard that it was said to those of ancient times . . . but I say to you. . . ." It is tempting to contrast the interpretation Jesus gives of a biblical passage with what one supposes is customary of his Jewish contemporaries. So, when Jesus, according to Matthew, puts forth an interpretation of "an eye for an eye and a tooth for a tooth," we tend to imagine violent retribution as the order of the day when Leviticus was written as well as in Jesus' own day (5:38). When Jesus forbids divorce, we suppose Jewish practices allowed men an easy dismissal of wives in the first century c.e. as well as several centuries earlier (5:31-32). Jesus emphasizes right motives in relationships. He connects anger toward a sibling to the commandment forbidding murder (5:22-23); he expands the commandment against adultery to include looking at a woman lustfully in one's heart (5:27-28). Do we conclude therefore that Jews of Jesus' day, like their ancestors, cared only about external conduct regardless of motives? The effect is to convey the replacement of a supposedly inferior Old Testament practice and, at the same time, a deficiency in first-century Judaism.

Judaism evolved and changed over the centuries. By the end of the first century, it was no longer a biblical religion. The Temple was gone, and with it the sacrificial cult and class of priests. New institutions replaced old, even before the destruction of the Temple. The synagogue, new methods of biblical interpretation, the Oral Torah, and new groups defining Jewish customs and observances emerged in the century before and after the birth of Jesus. Jews did not follow the Written Torah literally. They interpreted it. They interpreted "an eye for an eye" by assigning monetary value to an eye or a tooth and legislated damages accordingly. Laws regarding marriage were complex, arranged between families, and did not allow for the simple dismissal of a wife without cost to the husband. Jesus' ban on divorce did not liberate women over and against first-century practices in Judaism. And the notion that Jews did not care about motives is unfounded. It is not true in the Older Testament and it does not characterize Judaism. The rabbinic literature emphasizes the relationship between motive and action, and it is not a new concept of later generations of teachers.[9]

So, how are we to read these "antitheses"? We might begin by renaming them, and by putting them within the context of the ongoing interpretation of sacred texts. Jesus' statements are not really antithetical to anything. What is put forth, rather, is a new interpretation. This is what the Scripture says . . . and this is what it means. It is very similar to a later rabbinic method of interpretation: "You have read this . . . but the meaning is this. . . ."[10] Matthew's Jesus interprets the Scriptures for the Matthean community. The Gospel writer appealed to the authority of Jesus as an interpreter of Israel's Scriptures to guide and define the community. Other Jewish groups were also engaged in interpreting the Scriptures. The primary competition for the Matthean community was the Pharisees, and they were not biblical literalists. We will learn more about the historical Pharisees in the next chapter, but suffice it to say here that they were innovative teachers of the Oral Torah, known for righteousness in Torah observance, as Matthew tells us (5:20).

The more we know about early Judaism and its customs, the better equipped we are to correct the tendency to contrast Jesus' teaching with antiquated Older Testament customs. But whether we are familiar with first-century Jewish customs or not, we can reasonably assume that Jewish life evolved and the interpretation of sacred texts along with it. We might recall, too, what we know from our own experience, that it is a dangerous thing to impute inconsistency between motives and actions to others without knowing them very well; certainly it would be even riskier to make assumptions about the motives of ancient peoples about whom we know very little. The wisdom in Jesus' interpretations of his Scriptures, according to the Gospels, does not require the creation of a foe or adversary for effective preaching.

When we encounter biblical citations in the Newer Testament, I recommend that we break the habit of referring to these as "quotations from the Old Testament." This reminds us that Jesus and Paul and the Gospel writers had no Old Testament. Of course, it is our Older Testament the writers cite, but it was not theirs. They had Scriptures that included Torah, Prophets, and other Writings. The Old Testament is a second-century label created to distinguish these Scriptures from a New Testament; Old Testament implies that there is a New Testament. The term *Old Testament* is anachronistic in a first-century context, and I think the elimination of its usage will help us to enter imaginatively into the diversity of scriptural interpretation in first-century Judaism.

The quotations of biblical prophecies, laws, and customs are the references in the Newer Testament that seem to invite us to contrast New with Old, but the Gospel writers also allude biblical themes and stories. These allusions provide opportunities for preachers to connect the two parts of our Christian Bible in positive ways. For example, Matthew's Gospel begins with a genealogy that names women among the "begats." This departure from conventional genealogies calls attention to moments in Israel's history in which God's relationship with Israel takes unpredictable paths. Thus the writer gives biblical precedence for God's unfolding promise in the unusual circumstances of Jesus' birth. Of course, we'll miss it unless we know the stories of Tamar and Rahab, Ruth and Bathsheba! While the genealogy is rarely preaching material, serious consideration of the beginning of Matthew might provide some insights for preaching on what follows.

Another example of an allusion to Scriptures appears in the account of Jesus' forty days in the wilderness. All three Synoptic Gospels include this story (though very abbreviated in Mark), and lectionaries assign it to the First Sunday in Lent. The allusion to Israel's forty years in the wilderness is unmistakable. I have often heard readings that force a contrast between Jesus' successful resistance to temptation and Israel's failures. There is no indication of this meaning in the Gospels, however. I like the way The Rev. Marianne Edgar Budde lifted up this biblical allusion in a homily at the beginning of Lent:

> *The forty days of Lent are patterned after the great biblical rhythms of forty—the forty years the people of Israel wandered in the wilderness before entering the promised land; the forty days Jesus spent in his own wilderness, prayer, fasting, and spiritual preparation before beginning his public ministry. Forty is a symbolic number in the Bible. It signifies a long time. Forty days is long enough that if we are to do anything consistently in that time, we will have to think about it. It will take effort and intention. . . . Yet forty days is not forever. Lent is a long enough period of time to get our attention, but not so long that we can't see past it.*[11]

The biblical metaphor effectively connects our own experience with that of Jesus, with covenant people throughout the history of Israel, and with centuries of generations of Christians who begin each year to prepare for Easter by observing Lent.

Scripture and Worship

The ways Christians have interpreted the Gospels' use of Israel's Scriptures perpetuate the traditional view that the New Testament supersedes the Old Testament. Another way that Christian practice implies the inferiority of our Older Testament Scriptures is the place we give it in our worship. In the traditional mass (Roman Catholic, Lutheran, and Episcopal), the reading of the first lesson is from the Older Testament, followed by an epistle reading, followed by a sequential hymn to prepare for the reading from a Gospel, for which all stand. Other traditions may or may not read from the First Testament. Most biblical preaching relates to the Gospel. Both liturgical customs and the neglect of the Older Testament for Christian preaching imply a low regard for these Scriptures. It is beyond the scope of our purposes here to address the supersessionism inherent in our liturgical practices, but selecting the first lectionary reading for the basis of sermons or offering a sermon series on selected Older Testament texts makes the point that the gospel is present in the Older Testament as well as in those books we name "the Gospel."

So, why do we not preach on Older Testament texts more often? I do not believe the reason is because most preachers consciously regard these Scriptures as inadequate sermon material apart from Newer Testament revelation, though this may be the view of some. I imagine that habit, customs, and congregational expectations may be the more likely contributing factors. Another, though, may be uncertainty concerning how to preach a Christian sermon on an Older Testament reading on its own, apart from its direct relationship to a Newer Testament reading or Christian doctrine.

My seminary education a few decades ago included a course offered by a distinguished visiting professor on preaching on the Old Testament. He insisted that a Christian sermon must be distinctively Christian, and he challenged us regularly, "How is your sermon on this text different from the one delivered in a synagogue?" I seriously considered the challenge, but I thought at the time that I would like to preach a sermon on Scriptures held in common with Jews that would be acceptable in a synagogue or temple as well as in a church. I still think that a sermon that conveys the good news of the one God who loves all Abraham's children, indeed all the families of the earth, would be a worthy sermon for Jews and Christians alike. The fact that the literature contained in our Older Testament is complete on its own as the *Tanak* of Jewish tradition leads me to recognize the self-sufficiency of these texts.

At the same time, Christians know God through what God has revealed in Jesus Christ. We cannot read our Scriptures, any part of them, apart from our own experience of knowing God through the stories of Jesus and the teaching about him in the Scriptures. Our Christian faith informs how we interpret the Scriptures of our Older Testament. But that does not mean that we retroject the historical Jesus or Christian doctrine anachronistically into earlier texts, nor do we attribute to our ancestors knowledge of Jesus. Neither do we judge the matriarchs and patriarchs and prophets as having a relationship with God deficient or lacking in some way because they did not know God's revelation in Jesus Christ. The challenge for the preacher in working with these texts is to be faithfully Christian without suggesting that the only purpose of the Old Testament is to point to its fulfillment in the New.

A useful guiding principle is to take a theocentric perspective of the Christian Scriptures. From beginning to end, Genesis to Revelation, the Scriptures tell the story of the God of Israel in covenantal relationship with God's people. The Gospels and the letters of Paul are, in the first place, about the God of Israel; the writers tell us about what God is doing in and for Israel through God's anointed One, Jesus of Nazareth. Contrast this with a christocentric perspective, a common Christian view that the history of God's relationship with Israel is from the beginning destined to lead to Jesus Christ and it continues in the church. A christocentric perspective inevitably limits the value of the Older Testament to its fulfillment in the Newer Testament, and the New covenant replaces the Old. Whether one embraces that theological interpretation of history or not, a christocentric perspective is the dominant Christian view of the Newer Testament. We suppose the subject is Jesus Christ; I propose that the primary subject of the Second Testament is the God of Israel. The authors saw the activity of God in Israel's history in Jesus,

God's Messiah. When we consciously affirm that God is the subject of all the Scriptures, we affirm also the unity of the Scriptures. A theocentric perspective acknowledges that the God of the older covenant and the God of the newer covenant is One. Further, God does not break promises. The biblical testimony reveals a God who is faithful and reliable, at the same time surprising and free. I believe that adopting a theocentric perspective for interpreting the Scriptures will prove not only useful for preaching from the Older Testament but will also provide a helpful antidote to supersessionism in relating the two Testaments of the Christian Bible.

Another good reason for choosing to preach on the Older Testament on occasion is that the Newer Testament presupposes knowledge of these Scriptures and continues the long history of God's relationship with Israel recorded in them. The Newer Testament centers on only a few decades of that history. The older sacred writings include over one thousand years of God's relationship with humankind. There are aspects of that relationship that receive little attention in the limited focus of the Newer Testament, not because they are unimportant but because they are taken for granted by the first-century writers. If we neglect preaching on Older Testament texts we likely neglect themes that occur there. For example, the Older Testament affirms the goodness of creation and the redemption of all of creation, not only humankind. This is not a prominent theme in the Newer Testament, yet God's love for the earth and all that God has created is certainly an important topic for Christians today. According to many Older Testament accounts, the relationship between God and God's people is frequently dialogical, often argumentative or confrontational. I think this reflects an intimacy in the relationship unlike what we read in the Newer Testament, and I find it refreshing and liberating. (I once began a sermon on Abraham's argument with God over the fate of Sodom by observing that Christians are much too polite with God!)

I include here a sermon on Gen. 15:1-12, 17-18 as an example of interpreting an Older Testament text on its own terms. My intent, in Abraham's one-sided conversation with God, was to encourage trust in God's fidelity when experience creates doubt, and faith when it is difficult to be patient. I also wanted to interpret the phrase "God reckoned it to him as righteousness" within the context of Genesis, a citation best known from Paul's use of it in Rom. 4:3 and Gal. 3:6.

My belief in God's incarnation in Jesus Christ is evident implicitly in Abraham's recommendation that God consider entering more intimately into the human condition.

My shield? My reward will be great? I'm supposed to believe that? You promised. You promised that I'd be a great nation, that I'd have lots of descendants, and I don't have one, not even a single heir. Don't be afraid, you say. Well, I am . . . I am afraid. I trusted you. I left everything behind, family, home, land, trusting your promise. I believed you. That's bad enough, but Sarai, she trusted me. And now she waits. And she wonders. She does not speak the words, but her eyes search for answers. Where is this God of yours, the God who does not keep promises?

Stars? Count the stars? I pour out my heart to you, ask for answers, and you tell me to count stars? Hmmm . . . there are many. The heavens are so vast. When I look up I see . . . how much I cannot see . . . I see the world as you must see. I am so small in this world, a tiny speck in the vast universe, and yet, yet you speak to me. You call me by name. You promise descendants, as many as the stars, more than I can count. . . .

Oh, Lord God, I do believe you. You have asked me to see the world through your eyes, and for these moments, standing here alone, under the star-filled heavens, I do believe you. But please, a sign, for the daytime, when I cannot see the stars, even though they are certainly there. (Funny, isn't it, to think about stars being there in the daytime.) A sign, please, so I know I've not believed in vain. Something for Sarai's sake so she, too, might have courage to believe.

A covenant. Yes that would be good, a sign of a covenant. OK . . . a heifer, a she-goat, ram, all three years old . . . got that . . . dove. . . . Say, while I'm doing this, I wonder, have you thought how very strange this is going to sound to those many descendants far into the future? I suppose you're right. They will have their own obstacles to belief and will need their own signs. The strange particulars of our covenant will be the least of their worries. Okay, let's see now, cut in two, this half over this. . . . I ask for a sign, and it seems like I'm doing all the work here. . . .

There. All is ready. While we're waiting to seal this covenant, this covenant between you, the Master of the Universe, and me, Abram of Ur of the Chaldeans (unlikely partners, are we not?), I've been thinking.

You know, you've shown me how the world looks from your perspective, but it's different for us, for Sarai and me. For us, our time is limited, and finite. So when time passes, we get older, and we are quite aware of what Sarai calls the "biological clock ticking." We become impatient and worried, and we succumb to nagging doubt. Your time does not run out, but ours does. For us it's not so easy to keep believing the promise when we wait and nothing happens.

You know, Friend (I think I may call you that), I wonder if you really understand what the world looks like and feels like from the human point of view. You might want to think about that in your future with all these descendants. They might not be as patient with you as I've been. Just a suggestion. But when they do believe, Lord God, when they do believe, as you have done with me, reckon it to them as righteousness. And now I must return to Sarai. She's waiting . . . waiting. . . .[12]

There are many good reasons to preach on Older Testament texts on occasion. When we choose to do so and allow these Scriptures to stand on their own, we enhance the legitimacy of these Scriptures as an important part of the Christian Bible.

Summary

The early church showed wisdom in claiming Israel's Scriptures in its canon of sacred writings. However, in separating the Christian Bible into two distinct parts, they created a problem that is still with us, which is how to define the connection between the two parts. Historically, the church described the relationship in terms of discontinuity, the New Covenant superseding the Old, replacing it in the history of God's relationship with Israel. While most mainstream Christian denominations formally reject supersessionism, our reading of the Scriptures often perpetuates the idea that the Newer Testament provides the one and only correct interpretation of the Older Testament texts. This perspective, of course, denies the legitimacy of Judaism and its history of biblical interpretation. When biblical interpreters recognize the possibility of diverse and legitimate readings of the Torah and the Prophets within the first-century world, I think we will discover new possibilities for understanding biblical texts that will enliven our preaching as well as counter the unintended anti-Judaism in sermons.

The Uniqueness of Jesus

The conventional account of the history and theology of Christian origins persists in spite of our best intentions and formal disclaimers regarding supersessionism because of our investment in the uniqueness of Jesus. Protecting the unique or distinctive characteristics of the historical Jesus is at the heart of the persistent, often unconscious, reading of Gospel texts at the expense of a deficient Judaism. We tend to look for some continuity between the historical person Jesus and Christian claims about Jesus the Christ, and that interest seems to require some way in which Jesus was in his life distinctively set apart from others. But so long as we insist that Jesus must have been unique, we will habitually look to the way(s) in which he differed from all other Jews in his time, and likely define him over and against Judaism. We see this tendency to seek distinctive qualities of Jesus among biblical scholars, theologians, preachers, and teachers, many of whom formally reject supersessionism and affirm the Jewishness of Jesus.

In the history of historical-Jesus research, spanning over a century, the criteria of dissimilarity has dominated scholarship. By applying the criteria of dissimilarity, scholars sought to establish the authentic historical Jesus by distinguishing him both from Judaism and the early church's claims about him. Obviously, this method is predisposed to place Jesus at odds with Judaism and other Jews of his own time.

In the first critical quest for the historical Jesus, beginning in the nineteenth century, a criterion of dissimilarity served to establish discontinuity between the historical Jesus and the exalted christological claims of the Church. So, researchers regarded as historically authentic the words and deeds of Jesus reported in the Gospels that were dissimilar from later Christian claims.[13] Scholars engaged in this quest, extending into the early twentieth century, assumed the discontinuity between Jesus and the Judaism of his time; they took for granted the criterion of dissimilarity from Judaism. They repeated conventional anti-Judaism to assert his uniqueness. They did not question either the anti-Judaism or the assumption of the uniqueness of Jesus. For example, German theologian Karl Keim described Jesus as "the fulfillment of Judaism for the triumph over Judaism."[14] Adolf von Harnack asserted that "Jesus

Christ's teaching will at once bring us by steps which, if few, will be great, to a height where its connection with Judaism is seen to be only a loose one, and most of the threads leading [back] from it into [his] 'contemporary history' become of no importance at all."[15] Adolf Jülicher described Jesus as "honest enough to acknowledge openly a greatness peculiar to himself alone, something incomparable," and, "once again and finally, miraculously characteristic of him was his Jewish conquest of all that was Jewish."[16]

The development and articulation of a method centered on the criteria of dissimilarity defined the "New Quest" for the historical Jesus for approximately three decades, beginning in the 1950s. Scholars authenticated the distinctiveness of the historical Jesus by eliminating anything from the Gospel traditions that derived from Judaism and anything that might be ascribed to the claims of the early church. They did not deny that Jesus may have used common Jewish expressions, but these did not contribute to the picture of the historical Jesus, because "we would not encounter the message that was distinctively his own, and that is what we are looking for."[17] While the motives of the first quest were to separate the historical Jesus from Christian dogma, the second quest was more interested in the continuity between Jesus and developing Christianity. Consequently, the criterion of dissimilarity from the early church was relativized, and the criterion of dissimilarity from Judaism was emphasized.[18] Scholars of this era methodically, intentionally set Jesus over and against Judaism. What is most authentic about the historical Jesus, in this quest, is that he is the antithesis of Judaism. In the opening chapter of the first volume of his New Testament theology, Rudolf Bultmann states:

> As interpretation of the will, the demand of God, Jesus' message is a great *protest against Jewish legalism* [*sic*]—i.e. against a form of piety which regards the will of God as expressed in the written Law and in the Tradition which interprets it, a piety which endeavors to win God's favor by the toil of minutely fulfilling the Law's stipulations.[19]

This definition of Judaism summed up as legalism, and God's rejection of it, is the beginning and the foundation for a two-volume New Testament theology of one of the most brilliant New Testament scholars of the last century. Bultmann himself did not approve of the endeavors of his students on the "New Quest," but his influence on it is undeniable.

It is impossible to overestimate the preeminence of German scholarship of this era. German universities had been intellectual centers for centuries, and German biblical scholarship dominated Western Christian theological education. Scholars engaged in the "New Quest" as it was called then; Ernst Käsemann, Hans Conzelmann, Ernst Haenchen, Martin Dibelius, and others, represented the very best in New Testament studies in the last century. Their contributions to scholarship extended beyond historical-Jesus research, but such research was foundational to their work. As Jesus was antithetical to Judaism, so Christianity in its origins was also the antithesis of Judaism. This is not new, of course, but these scholars gave respectability to the conventional story of origins with clearly articulated methods of investigation. Bultmann's view is no different than Jülicher's, that what was uniquely characteristic of Jesus was his "Jewish conquest of all that was Jewish," but he lends to it the credibility of scientific historical-critical methods. But Bultmann and his students did not base their understanding of Judaism on any primary Jewish texts. They relied on secondary sources, by Christians, for their conception of Judaism.[20] It is indeed disheartening to observe the stature of these scholars and the time and place they worked: the middle decades of the twentieth century in Germany.

The hegemony of German biblical scholarship declined in the latter part of the last century as English-speaking scholarship rose to primacy in establishing the questions and methods of biblical studies. The third quest for the historical Jesus emerged in England and the United States in the 1980s. Characteristics of this quest include a decline in dependence on the criteria of dissimilarity, an emphasis on Jesus *within* Judaism, and some expressed uneasiness with the pursuit of the uniqueness of Jesus.

In *Jesus and Judaism*, which appeared in 1985, E. P. Sanders observes difficulties with the criteria of dissimilarity. He notes the lack of knowledge of early Judaism as well as of the developing church in the latter part of the first century, which thus leads to questionable results. He claims that the "test of double dissimilarity" eliminates too much material, and that what remains is "biased toward uniqueness."[21] James Charlesworth is critical of the "preoccupation with the notion of uniqueness" that leads to separate

Jesus from early Judaism.[22] By using the method of dissimilarity, he contends there is "a tendency to portray Jesus as a non-Jew and as a leader without followers."[23] Bernard Lee, among others, advocates for better knowledge of early Judaism, particularly of Galilee in the time of Jesus. He also questions the value of searching for the uniqueness of the historical Jesus, arguing that this does not give us the answer to the distinctiveness of Christianity. Part of the answer lies in the "historical and cultural conditions that accompanied and facilitated the evolution of Christian communities as entities outside Judaism, events from about two generations after Jesus."[24]

These are representative voices of the third quest for the historical Jesus who advocate for a better knowledge of early Judaism and have contributed greatly to that effort. Most have moved away from the criteria of dissimilarity and suggest other methods of investigation. John Dominic Crossan proposes the criterion of adequacy instead of dissimilarity: What best explains what Jesus said or did that led to such diverse understandings about him?[25] Gerd Theissen and Dagmar Winter argue for replacing the criteria of dissimilarity with the criterion of historical plausibility, which allows for including "continuity as well as discontinuity, analogy as well as difference, agreement as well as contrast."[26] They cite the problem of anti-Judaism and insist that historical-Jesus research must integrate Jesus into the Judaism of his time. Marcus Borg notes the decline of dissimilarity as a primary method among scholars, especially in North America, and hypothesizes that most scholars will be "eclectic in making judgments about what goes back to Jesus rather than developing a rigorously methodical approach. What seems to count most is a reasonable case that the tradition is early, plus a sense of 'fittingness' into a setting that makes sense in the context of the pre-Easter Jesus."[27]

Objections to the method of dissimilarity, increased knowledge of early Judaism, and awareness of the anti-Jewish tendencies in the pursuit of the uniqueness of Jesus are certainly positive trends in biblical scholarship. Scholars engaged in the third quest offer an alternative to a supersessionist reading of the Gospels. Yet not all who are engaged in historical-Jesus research embrace the critique of the criteria of dissimilarity. This method continued to dominate the work of many members of the Jesus Seminar.[28] Others still insist that the dissimilarity criteria produce the most reliable results, which is the authentic historical Jesus. Those who defend this method typically equate authenticity with uniqueness.

While many have committed themselves to improving their knowledge of early Judaism through reading primary Jewish texts, others still depend on outdated Christian sources. Admittedly, it is not an easy task to acquire the skills needed to read the early rabbinic literature. But many primary sources, Jewish and others, were written in Greek, and much of it has been translated. Further, both Christian and Jewish scholars have written excellent resources on early Judaism. Still, there seems to be insufficient consideration of the diversity of early Judaism, and this continues to affect how researchers evaluate materials. For example, it is quite common to contrast Jesus, an individual, with the Pharisees, without any consideration of diverse views and observances among them,[29] or to identify a custom within Judaism that only Jesus rejects.

Notwithstanding the advances in contemporary historical-Jesus research, including available resources on early Judaism, the defense of the uniqueness of the historical Jesus continues in academic circles and in the preaching and teaching of theologically trained professionals. For example, a sermon published in *Homiletic* under the title "The Telephone Pole Problem," used the telephone pole as a metaphor for what must be changed or eliminated in order for something new to emerge. To illustrate the point from the ministry of Jesus, the preacher asserts that "Jesus was never afraid to chop down a telephone pole or two." For example, "Jesus knocks down the old law in order to replace it with a new love." And "The Jewish laws and customs that had been part and parcel of *every person's life at that point* [italics mine] were the telephone poles that needed to be cut down and removed."[30]

The theme of the sermon is one with which I wholeheartedly agree and have preached often: "we're charged with being guardians of the ancient faith, while being open to fresh expressions of that faith," and it is difficult to discern "how much to change and how much to preserve."[31] If that is the case, then it seems likely, does it not, that the same would have been true in the Judaism that Jesus knew? Even if one has little knowledge of first-century Judaism, a reasonable and more nuanced portrait is in order, if only out of consideration for Jesus' own family and friends. The way this sermon presents it, Judaism itself was the "telephone pole" Jesus cut down.

According to this sermon, there are in the church both "pole huggers and pole choppers," and the author promotes "pole choppers." Sadly, he himself proves here to be a "pole hugger," with respect to preserving the Christian tradition of supersessionism by contrasting Jesus with his own Judaism.

A recent issue of *The Living Pulpit* explores the subject of tolerance in several articles. John W. Wimberly Jr., in "Jesus: A Model of Tolerance or Intolerance?" shows Jesus to be a model for both. He defends Jesus' intolerance of the Pharisees: "[M]any of the rules and regulations created by the scribes and Pharisees created systemic injustices. They artificially and unnecessarily burdened believers. Jesus simply could not remain silent in the face of such an intolerable misuse of religion. He refused to tolerate the intolerable."[32] Wimberly gives no evidence for systemic injustice or artificiality; a literal reading of the Gospels is apparently his only source for his view of the Pharisees, though he does not cite any specific texts. He defines Jesus, an individual, over and against all the scribes and Pharisees who imposed intolerable injustices, and of those two groups, scribes and Pharisees, Jesus is justifiably intolerant.

In the same magazine, Joan Delaplane, O.P., in "Is Tolerance Christian?" interprets Jesus' encounter with the Canaanite woman, as told in Matt. 15:21-28. She begins by observing that, "As a good Jew, Jesus would have understood his responsibility before Yahweh to have little or nothing to do with the goyim." Through his exchange with the Canaanite woman, "Jesus' horizons are broadened beyond his own cultural and religious tradition." This is a very common reading of this story, one that overstates Jewish avoidance of interaction with Gentiles and contrasts Jesus' enlightened, tolerant view with narrow (implied intolerant) views imposed by Judaism. The point of the article is one I embrace, which is tolerance as an important step toward replacing divisions among us with an appreciation for our common humanity. Jesus' tolerance of the Canaanite woman provides an example. The conclusion of the article links tolerance "of each and every creature" with "a basic foundation for fulfillment of the greatest of God's commandments, love of God and love of neighbor as oneself."[33] I like the interpretation of this commandment. But why not connect this, the greatest of God's commandments (or at least one of them!), with Jesus' own culture and religious tradition? Love of God and love of neighbor is at the core of Jewish tradition. It is all too common to define Jesus' actions over and against Judaism when it serves our purposes and fail to notice when Jesus is firmly grounded in his religious tradition.

In yet another article on the topic of tolerance, Walter J. Burghardt, S.J., also presents Jesus as "an admirable mix of tolerance and intolerance." His portrayal of Jesus, however, captures the diversity presented within the Gospels. For example, he shows Jesus as both intolerant *and* tolerant of the Pharisees: "Jesus was hardly 'in sympathy' with the Pharisees. The 'woes' on 'hypocrites' in Matthew 23 make me wince whenever I read them. Yet, Jesus could accept an invitation to dine with Simon the Pharisee." Burghardt takes the same approach in showing Jesus' relationships with his friends as both "in sympathy with" and not, likewise not "in sympathy with" Roman rule, yet responding to the centurion's pleas. Further, he notes "some cumbersome baggage" Christians carry, beginning with intolerance that has been violent, including the Crusades, forced conversions of Jews, and restricting them to ghettos.[34] Burghardt presents Jesus as a model of both tolerance and intolerance without creating a caricature of Judaism and, further, reminds Christian readers of the history of Christian intolerance of the most violent kind against Jews. This is a good illustration of portraying Jesus as a model for Christian behavior without setting him apart from his own Judaism.

The Gospel narratives depicting controversies between Jesus and the Pharisees are the most common sources for disassociating Jesus from his Judaism. We will examine other sources defining the historical Pharisees in the following chapter, and expanding our knowledge of the Pharisees will help us avoid the familiar stereotypes in our preaching. At this point we simply observe that there was diversity among the Pharisees, that Jesus and the Pharisees likely had much in common, and that the Gospel stories emphasize the differences, though even in the Gospels the image of the Pharisees is not uniformly negative. Also, much of the controversy with the Pharisees dates from the time of the Gospel writers' communities late in the first century and not from Jesus' own ministry.

The inclination to establish Jesus' uniqueness and the continuity between the Jesus of history and Christian claims about him seems firmly fixed in Christian thinking. Perhaps it is more than an inclination. Maybe it is a need to justify our Christian beliefs.

Regardless of the motive, the persistence of the pursuit of the uniqueness of Jesus is intimately linked with anti-Judaism. David Efroymson's words are instructive as we reconsider the way we think about Jesus in Judaism:

> Christians need more fully to appreciate that we have all we need in Jesus and his vision of God and what God is doing, and what God wants in response. We do not need to "highlight" this, to make it seem somehow brighter by contrast with whatever alternate visions may have opposed, or not been persuaded by, his. . . . Those alternate visions deserve to be studied and understood, but for their own sake, not for what is allegedly "lacking" in them. We do not need "opponents" to make Jesus more believable, or more acceptable. If we understand the opposition we are richer for it. If we make Jesus and his vision dependent on "superiority" to the opposition, Jesus is trivialized and we are poorer for it.[35]

Process Theology

In the 1970s and 1980s, process theology emerged as a new and creative rethinking of the traditional doctrines of God. Based on the philosophy of Alfred North Whitehead, theologians challenged the classical understanding of God as omnipotent and omniscient. When process theology turned to the task of revisioning classical Christologies, however, they repeated conventional anti-Judaism in their portrayals of the historical Jesus.

Clark Williamson, in "Anti-Judaism in Process Christologies?" shows that, in varying degrees, the Christologies of well-known process theologians perpetuate supersessionist ideas in the way they define the meaning of Jesus.[36] Williamson cites a few who simply follow traditional Christian constructions of Judaism and define Jesus in contrast to the supposed Judaism of his day. For example, Peter Hamilton intentionally seeks to "pick out aspects of the gospel accounts of Jesus' conduct and teaching which are in sharp contrast to the current practice and teaching of his day"[37] and asserts that "it was Jesus' conduct . . . that led the Jewish leaders to destroy him."[38]

Most process Christologies that Williamson examines, however, explicitly place Jesus within early Judaism. Norman Pittenger clearly does this, and he offers a nonexclusivist Christology.[39] Yet Williamson wonders about Pittenger's use of the term "older Israel" into which Jesus was born and the church that Pittenger claims is brought into being by faith in him. In Williamson's judgment, Pittenger appears to affirm "a gentle kind of supersessionism according to which the historical Jesus selects and omits from his heritage and fulfills it by understanding it more profoundly, thus allowing into history the release of a new affection which transcends his heritage."[40] Lewis Ford describes Jesus as offering a "radically new way of experiencing God's sovereignty as the power of the future," power that was persuasive and lacking the coercive aspects of the way Israel previously experienced God.[41] Ford also relies upon the often-repeated claim that Jesus had an intimacy with God that was offensive in Jewish piety of his day.[42] John Cobb encourages Christianity's openness to pluralism, yet he asserts that "the central and decisive fact in the appearance of Jesus was the renewal of the sense of the present immediacy of God," in contrast to Judaism and Pharisaism where "God was silent and remote."[43] Cobb displays sensitivity to the history of Christian anti-Judaism,[44] yet asserts that Jesus transformed the Judaism of his own day,[45] and that "Judaism has been seriously inhibited by the rejection of Jesus."[46] Cobb advocates the transformation of Christianity to accept pluralism with a Christology that defines Jesus and Christianity as transcending Judaism.

Williamson identifies Schubert Ogden's Christology as exemplary in consistently rejecting the conventional distinctions of supersessionism (Old Testament and New Testament, law and gospel, prophecy and fulfillment) *and* the uniqueness of Jesus. Ogden constructs a Christology from a theocentric perspective. The God known in Jesus is the only God there is to know and can be known apart from Jesus Christ or the Christian proclamation.[47] Ogden is critical of Christian claims that make God's disclosure in Jesus of Nazareth an event that "becomes a condition apart from which God is not free to be a gracious God."[48]

Williamson clearly states that the theologians whom he critiques are not any guiltier of anti-Judaism than others. And it is also the case that many of them wrote in the early seventies, before the third quest for the historical Jesus raised questions about the criteria of dissimilarity, before scholarship on early Judaism was readily available. But Williamson shows that even with a theological method that is notably progressive, these theologians "seek to establish the empirical uniqueness of the historical Jesus by setting him over and against Judaism."[49] And many do so while at the same time affirming the Jewishness of Jesus and expressing sensitivity to the matter of supersessionism. Williamson challenges his colleagues: "Process theologians break with the classical doctrine of God. Should we not also break the grip which the *adversus Iudaeos* tradition has upon us?"[50] What is at stake here is the perpetuation of Christian anti-Judaism by students who, in their theological studies, are persuaded by such Christologies and will have their own inherited anti-Judaism legitimized in a theological method that in other ways challenges traditional Christian thought.

Liberation Theologies

Liberation theologies represent a particular challenge to dismantling supersessionism. Like most liberal Christians, I am sympathetic to the commitments of liberation theologians. I am indebted to them for their critique of Western, white, privileged Christian tradition, and the empowerment of marginalized peoples. But I am not the first to observe that supersessionism has accompanied liberation theologies from their beginnings. Perhaps it is understandable. Implicit in liberation thought is the question, Liberated from what? When that question is imposed on the Gospels, the obvious, uncritical answer is: liberated from the limitations of Judaism. There is an inherent contradiction, however, in addressing injustice at the expense of perpetuating another. It is troubling that those who are drawn to liberation theologies because of their own commitments to the poor and oppressed unwittingly have their own negative stereotypes of Jews and Judaism reinforced.[51]

Gustavo Gutíerrez, in his *Theology of Liberation*, asserts the common supersessionist theme that God has ended his covenant with the Jews because of their infidelity. The earliest liberationist writings were published in the 1970s, before much of the current scholarship on early Judaism challenged the conventional Christian construction of Judaism, but several prominent voices repeated the supersessionist views long after the critique of liberation theologies noted the problem. Gutíerrez repeats the supersessionist theme of his earlier publications in the recent anniversary edition of his work.[52] John Pawlikowski observed that Gutíerrez's Christology could be transformed to allow for authentic Judaism, in that liberation is linked to the exodus event, so it is especially disturbing when a new edition takes no account of advances in scholarship.[53]

Jon Sobrino and Leonardo Boff base their liberation theologies on the contrast between the "historical Jesus" and a distortion of early Judaism. In *Christology at the Crossroads*, Sobrino contrasts Jesus with the Gospels' portrait of the Pharisees in particular, and Judaism in general. For example: "Jesus presented people with a God who stands in complete contradiction to the existing religious situation. His God is distinct from, and greater than, the God of the Pharisees."[54] And he suggests that God "accepted Jesus' death on the cross so that he might overcome the old religious schema once and for all. . . ."[55] In *Jesus the Liberator*, written fourteen years after the first book, Sobrino repeats the same judgments of the "mechanisms of oppressive religion" that Jesus "unmasked."[56] He identifies the Pharisees and scribes, priests and rulers, and the rich (Jews, implied) as oppressors and "anti-Kingdom," denounced by Jesus.[57] The subtitle of Sobrino's "new" Christology (he acknowledges that there is little that is new or original) is "A Historical-Theological View." But there is no consideration of engagement with any scholarship on the historical Jesus or on early Judaism. Boff's depiction of Judaism is similar to Sobrino's, including such inaccuracies as defining the essence of postexilic Judaism in observance of the Law, that Jews discriminated between those whom God did and did not love, and that Judaism encouraged hate toward one's enemy. About the Pharisees he says: "The Pharisees had a morbid conception of God. Their God no longer spoke to human beings. Their God had left them a Law."[58]

Sobrino asserts that, in Latin America, the question is not "how to do theology *after* Auschwitz but doing it *in* Auschwitz."[59] But must it be one or the other? *Can* it be one or the other? At the core of liberation theologies is solidarity with those who suffer violence, who live in poverty, who live on the margins of society, who are dehumanized, who experience injustice. And supersessionism is an injustice that has had tragic consequences. As long as Christians dismiss the role of supersessionism in creating an environment for the Holocaust, we are never safely beyond Auschwitz. True liberation cannot dismiss this injustice or trivialize it.

Feminist Theology

Feminist theology belongs under the umbrella of liberation theologies. The presence of supersessionist themes in feminist theology has been particularly distressing, because Christian and Jewish feminists have in common the problem of naming patriarchal systems of injustice in our respective traditions. But in the quest for liberation from patriarchy, Christian feminists adopted themes from conventional Christian anti-Judaism. Two prominent themes in feminist theology include the negative view of the God of the Older Testament and portraying Jesus in contrast to early Judaism.

Feminist writers have blamed Judaism for the origin of patriarchy, charging that the ancient Israelites replaced goddess worship with the jealous, warrior, Father God. They developed this theme from research conducted in Near Eastern studies of female deities and goddess worship in the ancient world.[60] And they expanded on it, attributing to the goddess the values of feminism and the tyranny of patriarchy to the God of the Old Testament and to Judaism. Patriarchal monotheism, according to this theory, legitimates violence and oppression.[61] This theme echoes the common motif of the God of wrath of the Old Testament who condones violence, contrasted with the God of love made known in Jesus Christ.

Defining the uniqueness of Jesus over and against Judaism takes on a feminist twist in portraying Jesus as the first feminist. In his article "Jesus Was a Feminist," Leonard Swidler claims that the status of women in Palestine in Jesus' time heightens the impact of Jesus' positive treatment of women. He appeals to rabbinic literature to demonstrate the extreme inferiority in Judaism: the prayer in which men thanked God they were not created women, the admonition not to speak to women in public, the shame of teaching Torah to a woman, the value of women as confined to childbearing and child-rearing, to name a few examples.[62] These often-repeated descriptions of the bleak situation of Jewish women at the time of Jesus have entered into the evidence for Jesus as a champion of the cause of feminism. The supposition that Judaism, in particular, oppressed women plays out in feminist theology as a foil to Jesus' liberation of women.

There are several methodological problems with this construction of the status of women in Judaism at the time of Judaism. First, the selected evidence from rabbinic literature all post-dates Jesus.

Most comes from the Babylonian Talmud, a document compiled in the sixth century. The rabbinate as an institution did not exist at the time of Jesus, and it took a long time for the views of the rabbis to represent anything more than a minority opinion. Second, rabbinic pronouncements about women do not necessarily reflect the real lives of women in society. Comparing the words and deeds of Jesus to the later rabbis involves "comparing the words and attitudes of an itinerant preacher with laws and sayings formulated in the rarefied atmosphere of rabbinic academies."[63] There is a hypothetical nature to rabbinic legal discussions, compared to Jesus' actual involvement with women. Third, the rabbinic literature also includes positive views of women and anecdotes of compassion and sensitivity, and when given a contextual reading may reflect a development of rabbinic thought indicating concern for improving the situation of women.[64] Finally, to give Christian feminists better perspective, the rabbinic literature is most appropriately compared with the writings of the early church fathers.

In the case of feminist theology, the criticisms came first from Jewish feminists, charging Christians with not only sloppy scholarship but with a failure of the feminist ethic. Though early critique was hard to hear, Marianne Grohmann observes: "For so young a theology as the feminist one, it is especially astonishing how quickly it is ready for self-criticism and working on a revision of their conditions, which does not operate at the expense of Judaism."[65] Jewish and Christian feminist scholars in America and Europe held conferences, published responses to each other's critiques, and raised awareness of the presence of supersessionism. Undoubtedly the themes were so very familiar to Christian feminists they appropriated them unwittingly.

I cannot cite Swidler's article, "Jesus Was a Feminist," which appeared in 1971, without a word of appreciation for our feminist brother. It is impossible to underestimate how important Swidler's article was to so many Christian women in those days, notwithstanding the dependence on the caricature of Jewish life. But we are most indebted to Swidler for his enormous contributions to Jewish-Christian relations over the last decades. He would not write the same article today with its caricature of life in first-century Judaism. He has a long history of commitment to Jewish-Christian relations, and his publications and essays have made knowledge of the Pharisees and of early Judaism at the time of Jesus readily accessible for lay audiences.

Liberation Theology without Supersessionism

We call attention to liberation theologians not because they are guiltier of perpetuating supersessionism than others, but because church leaders who are drawn to liberation theologies are also most likely formally to reject supersessionism. Seminary students who gravitate toward courses in liberation theology and those offering a liberationist perspective on biblical studies are the same ones who are apt to enroll in the course I teach on interpreting the Bible after the Holocaust. Without exception, those who criticize liberation theologians are sympathetic to their commitments and the passion for justice. Unfortunately, liberationist writings reinforce the deeply ingrained historical inaccuracies and stereotypes of Judaism among those most likely open to raising their awareness of supersessionism and its falseness.

Liberation theologies need not depend on an inferior Judaism. One can speak eloquently of Jesus the liberator without denigrating Jesus' own Jewish life. As Mary Boys puts it, "Commitment to the way of Jesus cannot come at the expense of deprecating the people from whom Jesus came."[66] Christian feminists have responded to the critique of Jewish feminists, though the image of Jesus as liberator of women from Jewish patriarchy persists in popular Christian feminism. Criticism of the themes of supersessionism found in liberation theologies does not require a rejection of what these theologies offer us. Our task is to learn to recognize supersessionism wherever it occurs, name it, and refuse to repeat it.

In the following sermon on Jesus' visit to the home of Martha and Mary (Luke 10:38-42), I try to show that the liberating gospel need not pit Jesus against a caricature of Jewish life. I use an imaginative reading of the story to communicate liberating themes in a way that is consistent with the realities of first-century life in the time of Jesus and is consistent also within Luke's Gospel:

How did he say it? What was his tone? Annoyed? "Martha, Martha, you are worried and distracted by many tasks; there is need of only one thing. Mary has chosen the better part, which will not be taken away from her." Patronizing? "Martha, Martha. . . ." Or gentle?

This little episode, which takes place on the journey to Jerusalem in Luke's Gospel, has received a lot of attention in feminist interpretations in the last few decades. In the early '70s, Jesus' affirmation of Mary, who chose to sit with the other disciples and learn, represented Jesus' validation of women's ministry beyond the traditional subservient roles, according to feminist readings. Leonard Swidler wrote an article with the title "Jesus Was a Feminist," and Jesus' approval of Mary over Martha supported his thesis. But in the next wave of feminism, women spoke more of solidarity and respecting each other's choices, at home and at church. And whatever we decide about Jesus' tone of voice, we might empathize a bit with Martha. If we're honest, we might also be a little uneasy with the way Jesus appears to pit the two sisters against each other. After all, Martha is tending to hospitality for her guests. And as much as we may enjoy the idea, we must acknowledge the anachronism in calling Jesus a feminist. That takes him completely out of the world in which he lived.

I imagine that the meaning of the story in Luke's Gospel was quite simple to earlier readers. It is placed within the long journey narrative of Luke that began at the end of the last chapter, where Jesus "sets his face to go to Jerusalem." And he is very direct about the single-minded commitment required of those who choose to follow him. Let the dead bury their own dead. No looking back. Take no provisions. Depend on the hospitality of others. So here, we have another incident that makes the point about priorities, setting aside anything that distracts from the journey. But, it's hard for us to hear that, because our ears hear some dissonance, however we hear Jesus' words to Martha.

So, let's turn to a time-honored tradition, a method of interpreting the Scriptures that is as old as the Scriptures themselves, which is retelling the stories for new audiences in new circumstances. I think this one needs some reframing for us to hear it.

It was late afternoon, and Jesus and his disciples were talking about where they might find lodging for the night. Jesus recalled that old family friends lived in a nearby village, and he suggested that they might know of a place to stay. "I'd love to see Mary and Martha again," he told his friend. "I haven't seen them since Mary's wedding. Mary's a widow now. She lives with her sister. Martha manages a small vineyard on the edge of the village. I think we'll probably find her there when we get into town."

And they did. Martha was delighted to see her friend Jesus. "You must stay with us," she said, "We'll have dinner together and time to catch up on all the news. There really is no place to stay in our village, and it is much too dangerous for you to travel at night. The Roman occupiers have a habit of harassing strangers, or worse."

"Won't you be in danger for providing lodging for us?" Jesus asked.

"No. I don't think so. Mary and I are known here, and they leave us alone. Oh, Mary will be so happy to see you! She'll be home by now. Why don't you go ahead and I'll be there soon."

When Martha arrived at home, she found Mary with their guests, already engaged in conversation. She waved a greeting rather than interrupting and went off to begin preparations for the unexpected guests. A couple of times, she came to the door to get Mary's attention to come help. Mary nodded, indicating she would be right there. Finally, Martha, a bit exasperated, did interrupt. "Jesus, dear friend, would you please tell my sister to come give me a hand?"

"Oh-oh," Jesus said to himself. "I'll offend them both if I'm not careful."

And to Martha, he said, "Martha, I'm so sorry. It isn't Mary's fault. We got involved in our conversation. What can we do to help? We can talk in the kitchen and then over dinner. [Okay, that might be a stretch, but isn't it a nice thought?] Besides, I want you both to hear about the journey we are on."

As they sat around the table, Jesus spoke to them about his sense of God's kingdom, beginning with those who are most oppressed by the current occupation, those who had lost their land, those burdened by enormous taxation. A grassroots movement.

"God's kingdom? The Romans won't like to hear that. They think they rule the world," Martha said bitterly.

"They do. This is about refusing to live in fear, Martha. And it's about healing. I have so many wonderful stories to tell."

Mary nudged Martha. "See why I couldn't tear myself away?" Mary whispered to Martha. Martha smiled and nodded. I understand.

Jesus spoke with urgency and passion, yet quietly, without raising his voice, with a compelling authority, the kind that is spirit filled. His friends, too, spoke with energy and commitment as they told about changed lives, their own and the lives of others on this journey. They talked well into the night, of family news and mutual friends, about agitation among some Jews in Galilee for revolt, about unrest in Jerusa-

lem, confiscation of land in Galilee, about finding another way besides armed revolt. Finally Jesus said, "We can't continue our journey unless we get some rest."

The next morning, as Jesus and his companions prepared to go on their way, Martha said, "We never asked where you are going."

"Jerusalem."

"No! No, don't!" Martha pleaded. "The situation there is so volatile these days. There is such hostility, especially for non-residents. It's too dangerous."

"But we must. The movement of the kingdom of God must lead to Jerusalem."

"I fear for your life," Mary said quietly.

"I know," Jesus told her, "but we can't let our fears hold us back."

"Shalom, dear friends. God go with you," the women said. "God be with you." They turned to go on their way, toward Jerusalem. Then Jesus turned back and, looking at Mary and Martha standing at the gate, he spoke to them. "Mary, Martha, won't you come with us?"[67]

Winners and Losers

"Why does someone have to win?" Seminary president and pastoral theologian Keith A. Russell poses this question and observes that in both our national life and in our churches we operate with a win/lose paradigm. Our debates over issues assume that someone must win and, therefore, someone must lose, and there seems to be no room for difference or disagreement. Russell points out the obvious, that a win/lose paradigm significantly constrains interfaith relationships: "If we Christians need to win, can we ever respect the beliefs of Muslims or Hindus? How do we relate to Judaism, and how do we relate to our long and shameful history of anti-Semitism?"[68]

Christian supersessionism relies on a win/lose paradigm. The conventional story of origins establishes the success of Christianity by asserting the failure of Judaism. This paradigm informs the way we have traditionally read our Scriptures, constructed our theologies, and defined our history, and it is deeply embedded in our Christian identity. But it is time for a paradigm shift. In the first place, the prevailing paradigm is not historically accurate. Second, it distorts our Scriptures. And finally, the ideology of winning, thus creating an "other" that must lose, does not serve us well. Authentic

Christianity does not require the displacement of Judaism. Effective proclamation does not depend on an inferior "other." Christianity can make room for Judaism in its story of origins. One might argue that it must.

It is time for a paradigm shift, but such a shift is not easy to make. The first step toward addressing Christian supersessionism may be the acknowledgment that it preserves a win/lose paradigm, a paradigm that requires that someone must lose. If we are honest, we must admit that winning is more satisfying than losing, and that some of our resistance to rethinking how we tell our story of origins and how we interpret our Scriptures may be attributed to the fact that the traditional story line confirms that we are right. The New Testament provides the right interpretation of the Old Testament. Jesus was right and the Pharisees were wrong. Christianity superseded a defective Judaism in God's salvation history, and therefore its success was divinely ordained. There is an appeal to the familiar story because it validates our convictions.

Barbara Brown Taylor describes how reading the biblical story preserves our sense that God favors us to the exclusion of others and how appealing this is:

> Since the Bible contains the foundational stories of two distinct faiths it is chock full of attacks on those outside the fold. Sometimes the attacks are sanctioned by God and other times they erupt out of pure human meanness, but in either case they come as no real surprise. When any group of people is trying to discover who they are, they usually begin by declaring who they are *not*: we are not Canaanites, not Samaritans, not Pharisees, not Romans, not Greeks, *not them*.
>
> These are satisfying parts of the story to tell around the campfire, because they reinforce the boundaries of the group as well as its rightness. . . . The Egyptians are drowned in the sea. Jesus turns over the tables in the temple. No one comes to the Father but by me. If these stories are beloved, then at least one reason is because they guarantee the privileges of those who tell them.[69]

She reminds us, though, that the Bible also includes stories in which God works outside the fold, outside the community. Christians have woven those parts of the biblical narrative into our story of origins, identifying with the outsiders that were included and, in telling our story, project onto Judaism the failure to recognize that God is not bound by human definitions of who belongs and who does not. Unfortunately, we have presumed that the story ends there, with Christians getting it right and Jews rejected because of their own misunderstanding. Taylor reminds us, though, that this is a "Never-Ending Story," and "that God's plot is always larger than the ones we weave to reassure ourselves, and that even when we say the story's over, the story's not over. As long as anyone is alive to play a part or talk about it afterwards, the sacred narrative continues—at least until the day we wake from sleep to find that there is room in God's story for us all."[70]

The attraction of the conventional story in which we are winners is undeniable, but the consequence of perpetuating supersessionism is that we leave no room in God's story for Judaism. And I do not believe that is the story we want to tell.

Those of us who regularly tell the "never-ending story" in the form of sermons can take steps toward replacing the conventional story of Christian supersessionism by first of all resolving not to repeat negative views of Judaism, even when the biblical texts appear to support it. Remember that the Gospel narratives are told from the point of view of those who later became Christians; they do not give an unbiased historical portrait of *other* groups within Judaism. And remember, too, that Paul and the Gospel authors interpreted their Scriptures (which we now call our Older Testament) among others engaged in the same task. When we think in terms of multiple interpretations among first-century Jews rather than one right interpretation, we recognize that the Newer Testament writers were not simply stating the obvious, or that others were incapable of interpreting their Scriptures. Finally, the more informed we are about first-century Judaism (and Judaism today, too!) the better equipped we are to read the Gospel narratives in light of the diversity of early Judaism. We will be more able to recognize the caricatures that perpetuate the preaching and teaching of contempt against Judaism.

3

The Pharisees and the Law

"Woe to you, scribes and Pharisees, hypocrites! For you tithe mint, dill and cummin, and have neglected the weightier matters of the law: justice and mercy and faith. . . . Woe to you, scribes and Pharisees, hypocrites! For you clean the outside of the cup and of the plate, but inside they are full of greed and self-indulgence. . . . Woe to you, scribes and Pharisees, hypocrites! For you are like whitewashed tombs, which on the outside look beautiful, but inside they are full of the bones of the dead and of all kinds of filth. So you also on the outside look righteous to others, but inside you are full of hypocrisy and lawlessness." (Matt. 23:23, 25, 27)

NO WONDER READERS OF THE NEWER TESTAMENT think the Pharisees were the epitome of religious hypocrisy! Jesus, according to Matthew, condemns them in a lengthy litany of faults extending nearly all of chapter 23. According to Mark, the Pharisees conspire against Jesus following a Sabbath healing with intent to destroy him (3:1-6), and Jesus charges the Pharisees with hypocrisy, quotes Scripture against them, and accuses them, "You abandon the commandment of God and hold to human tradition" (7:8). Luke's parable of the Pharisee and the tax collector presents the Pharisees as contemptuous of others and as engaging in self-serving prayer (18:9-14). Christians who rely on the Newer Testament as their only source of information are of course more likely to regard the Pharisees with contempt. According to the Synoptic Gospels, the Pharisees are opponents of Jesus and the disciples are indicted for religious hypocrisy, charged with observing the Law at the expense of human compassion, and criticized for obsessive concern with image and position.

It is hardly surprising, therefore, that sermons typically present the Pharisees in the same way they appear in the Gospels.

While understandable, this portrayal of the Pharisees from the pulpit has serious consequences. First, it misrepresents the Pharisees and their Oral Law and, since they are the primary representatives of Judaism in the Gospels, misrepresents Judaism itself. Second, it also conveys a misunderstanding of the teachings of Jesus as well as the teachings and origin of the early church. In the introduction to Leo Baeck's book, *The Pharisees and Other Essays*, Krister Stendahl writes:

> Who were the Pharisees? This question is of paramount significance to both Judaism and Christianity. It could be argued that it is of even greater significance for Christianity, since the teaching of Jesus and much early Christian material is available to us only in its sharp critique of and contrast to the Pharisees. Every misunderstanding of Pharisaism hence brings with it a misconception of the aims and intentions of early Christianity.[1]

In addition to perpetuating anti-Judaism, the way we speak of the Pharisees in our preaching affects our understanding of the Gospels and an appreciation for the real first-century controversies that led to the emergence of Christianity.

In this chapter, we will examine primary sources toward reconstructing a historically reliable definition of the first-century Pharisees. Included in this historical definition is a discussion of the Pharisaic Oral Torah (Law). This is the first step toward correcting the Christian caricature of the Pharisees and a common misperception of the Law. Next, we will look at the Synoptic Gospels within their late first-century context, at the time they were written. The polemic against the Pharisees belongs within this context, a part of intra-Jewish controversy over the future of Israel. And we will observe that the Gospels do not present a uniformly hostile view toward the Pharisees. The picture is more complex than traditional Christian bias allows. Finally, I will identify some of the more common and often subtle ways preachers perpetuate the stereotype of Pharisees and the Law so that we learn to recognize them. Drawing from the historical definition of the Pharisees and placing the Gospels in their late first-century context, I offer some strategies for rehabilitating the Pharisees in Christian preaching.

Who Were the Pharisees?

There are three primary sources dating from the historical period of our inquiry that provide information on the Pharisees. Unfortunately, none of these sources has as its main purpose describing the Pharisees, and each one has an agenda that affects what it says about the Pharisees. Josephus describes the Pharisees in both *The Jewish War* and *Jewish Antiquities*. His very flattering portrayal may be attributed to his intent to present them as the legitimate representatives of Judaism following the Jewish War and the destruction of the Temple in 70 C.E. The *Mishnah*, the earliest written compilation of Oral Torah in the early third century C.E., contains traditions of the Pharisees from the first century. In the *Mishnah*, it is difficult to determine the extent to which later redactions have affected the transmission of earlier debates and opinions. Also, because the rabbis regarded themselves as successors to the Pharisees, they assumed both knowledge about them and a positive view toward them. The Newer Testament is also a primary source, especially the Synoptic Gospels.[2] Of the three primary sources, the Gospels devote proportionately the most attention to the Pharisees, but in these narratives they usually play the role of antagonists to Jesus and the disciples. It is important to note that all three primary sources were written after the destruction of the Temple.

Until the 1970s, definitions of the Pharisees betrayed confessional interests. Jewish scholars were interested primarily in the continuity between the Pharisees and the origin of rabbinic Judaism, and the early rabbinic literature was the only relevant primary source. Christian scholars relied on the Gospels to define the Pharisees. If they considered other sources, it was to confirm what was "known" from the Newer Testament, especially the Gospels.

Two Views of the Pharisees

In the 1970s, two Jewish scholars produced significant scholarship on the historical Pharisees, investigating the primary sources and employing critical methods of study. Jacob Neusner was interested in the historical Pharisees prior to the year 70 C.E., particularly Hillel.[3] The title of Neusner's comprehensive study, *Rabbinic Traditions about the Pharisees before 70 A.D.*,[4] implies his skepticism about what can be known about the Pharisees before the destruction of the

Temple. (We have only what later generations say about them; we have no sources deriving from the Pharisees themselves.) Neusner's *From Politics to Piety: The Emergence of Pharisaic Judaism* made his work on the Pharisees accessible to nonspecialists, and here he constructs his definition of the historical Pharisees on the basis of all three primary sources.[5] Ellis Rivkin, in *A Hidden Revolution: The Pharisees' Search for the Kingdom Within*, is more confident than Neusner about the reliability of the historical documents and less concerned with the impact of the destruction of the Temple.[6] Rivkin and Neusner investigate the same sources but emerge with different historical constructions of the Pharisees.

According to Neusner, the Pharisees were an influential political party during the Hasmonean period following the Maccabean revolt in 166 B.C.E. Toward the end of the Hasmonean rule, as they were losing political sway, they focused on the observance of the ancestral laws, particularly the ritual purity laws, which, in the Written Torah, were applicable only to the priests. During most of the first century, the Pharisees were a table-fellowship sect defined by their observance of the purity laws. Following the war against Rome in 70 C.E., the Pharisees emerged again in the political arena with the responsibility for managing internal affairs and establishing stability under Rome in the wake of the war's devastation in Galilee and Judea. In this capacity they were also leaders in defining Judaism around Torah observance.[7] The title of Neusner's book indicates the shifts in roles and emphases of the historical Pharisees: *From Politics to Piety*, with the subtitle *The Emergence of Pharisaic Judaism*.

Neusner's definition of the Pharisees originates in the analysis of rabbinic texts. In this large and complex body of literature, *perushim*, translated "Pharisees," has different meanings. In some contexts, *perushim*, which literally means "separatists," clearly refers to the group within early Judaism known as the Pharisees. In other contexts the term clearly does not, and it should be transliterated with a lowercase "p." In yet other occurrences it is not certain whether *perushim* is a proper name, whether it refers to the Pharisees or not. In other words, it is not clear whether to translate (or transliterate) with an uppercase "P" or lowercase "p." Neusner makes the judgment that those ambiguous occurrences do refer to Pharisees and he included them in his definition of the Pharisees. These texts lend weight to the picture of the Pharisees as a table-fellowship sect set apart from others by their concern with observing ritual purity laws.

He finds the Gospel texts confirming the portrayal of the Pharisees derived from the rabbinic literature. The polemic in the Gospel texts frequently relate to Pharisaic observance of ritual purity laws and objections to Jesus and his disciples eating with tax collectors and sinners, that is, those who do not observe these laws.

Neusner attributes Josephus's flattering descriptions of the Pharisees to apologetics. In *Jewish War* Josephus describes them this way:

> The Pharisees are the most accurate interpreters of the laws, and hold the position of the leading sect. . . . they hold that to act rightly or otherwise rests, indeed, for the most part with men, but that in each action Fate cooperates.[8]

He contrasts them with the Sadducees in claiming that they "are affectionate with each other and cultivate harmonious relations with the community."[9] Josephus also contrasts the Pharisees and Sadducees in *Jewish Antiquities*:

> The Pharisees had passed on to the people certain regulations handed down by former generations and not recorded in the Laws of Moses, for which reason they are rejected by the Sadducean group, who hold that only those regulations should be considered valid which were written down (in Scripture), and that those which had been handed down by former generations need not be observed. And concerning these matters the two parties came to have controversies and serious differences, the Sadducees having the confidence of the wealthy alone but no following among the populace, while the Pharisees have the support of the masses.[10]

Josephus describes the Pharisees this way in *Jewish Antiquities*:

> The Pharisees simplify their standard of living, making no concession to luxury. They follow the guidance of that which their doctrine has selected and transmitted as good, attaching the chief importance to the observance of those commandments which it has seen fit to dictate to them. They show respect and deference to their elders, nor do they rashly presume to contradict their proposals.[11]

Following a brief description of some of their beliefs, Josephus says:

> Because of these views they are, as a matter of fact, extremely influential among the townsfolk and all prayers and sacred rites of divine worship are performed according to their exposition. This is the great tribute that the inhabitants of the cities, by practicing the highest ideals both in their way of living and in their discourse, have paid to the excellence of the Pharisees.[12]

Neusner asserts that in these passages Josephus directs his description of the Pharisees to a Roman audience to make the case that the Pharisees were the best candidates for managing internal affairs and restoring stability after the war. Josephus's claim to have been a Pharisee himself is also part of a Roman apologetic.[13] Josephus's account of the Pharisees as significant role-players in the Hasmonean dynasty supports Neusner's view of the Pharisees before the Common Era.

Rivkin's interest is in the origin of the Pharisees. His analysis of the primary sources leads to the conclusion that the origin of the Pharisees constituted what he calls a *hidden revolution*. The emergence of the Pharisees is hidden in that there is no evidence of the existence of Pharisees before the Maccabean Revolt, and they are present in the Hasmonean dynasty as an influential group following the revolt, exercising both political and religious leadership. Their rise to popularity was revolutionary because they redefined Judaism. The Pharisees established the authority of the Oral Torah alongside the Written Torah, and they appropriated priestly observances for the people. With the ascendancy of the divinely revealed twofold Law (written and oral), the literal reading of the Written Law would never again stand apart from the Oral Law and its continual interpretation.[14]

Rivkin takes Josephus at his word, that "the Pharisees are the most accurate interpreters of the Law and hold the position of the leading sect (*sic*)."[15] He does not question the authenticity of Josephus's description of the Pharisees as extremely popular and respected interpreters of sacred rites, so much so that even the Sadducees, who held only to the literal Written Torah, submitted "to the formulas of the Pharisees, since otherwise the masses would not tolerate them."[16] He accepts the reliability of Josephus's account of his own identity as a Pharisee. Rivkin thinks it is improbable that Josephus exaggerated the popularity of the Pharisees to convince a Roman audience that the Pharisees were the preferred candidates for oversight of internal affairs after the war against Rome, since Josephus devotes relatively little space to the Pharisees in his two major works. Josephus actually gives much more attention to describing the Essenes!

With respect to the rabbinic literature, Rivkin includes only those texts in which *perushim* unambiguously refers to the Pharisees, texts in which they are contrasted with the Sadducees over legal disputes. He excludes the more ambiguous passages where it is not certain whether an uppercase "P" or lowercase "p" is intended, and in doing so eliminates from his definition texts that characterize the group as separating themselves from nonobservant people.

Rivkin finds support in the Newer Testament that the Pharisees were the authoritative interpreters of the Oral Law. According to Matthew, "The scribes and Pharisees sit on Moses' seat; therefore, do whatever they teach you and follow it" (23:2-3a). Criticisms of the Pharisees in the Gospels typically involve observance and interpretations of legal matters. Paul claims to be "as to the law, a Pharisee" and "as to righteousness under the law, blameless" (Phil. 3:5b; 6b). Rivkin includes texts naming scribes and lawyers along with Pharisees in his reading of the Gospels. The scribes and Pharisees are so often named together that he believes the Gospel authors did not distinguish between them; neither did they distinguish Pharisees from lawyers. This enhances his definition of the Pharisees as a scholar class and acknowledged interpreters of the Oral Torah. He does not believe that the few accounts of the Pharisees criticizing Jesus and his disciples for eating with tax collectors and sinners indicate that they habitually separated themselves from the wider population.

Newer Testament interpreters who recognize the need for a historically reliable definition of the Pharisees tend to adopt a description that best suits their preference without considering whether it is the best reading of the primary documents. Neusner's definition has appealed to many Christian scholars because it is very similar to the prevailing view that the Pharisees in Jesus' time separated themselves from others by the strict observance of ritual purity laws. And

Rivkin's definition works well for those who seek to counter the negative Christian stereotype of the Pharisees.

Rivkin and Neusner each offer a defensible and plausible definition of the Pharisees based on the same primary sources. And they differ significantly on several points. Rather than choosing one or the other, I suggest we consider the following questions in order to construct an operating definition of the historical Pharisees: Are there points of convergence in competing definitions? Where do they agree? Are the differences irreconcilable? What historical period is of most interest? Interpreters of Gospel texts must decide whether to focus on the Pharisees in the time of Jesus or in the time of the Gospel writers and their communities. What aspects of the Pharisees are most significant?

Neusner's observation that the rabbinic literature discloses more about the rabbis at the time of composition than about the Pharisees of the first century is comparable to what we have observed about the Gospels, which tell us more about the writers and their communities after the destruction of the Temple than they reveal about the historical Jesus. It is a common view, as we noted above, that the controversies with the Pharisees reveal conflicts between the early believers and the Pharisees in the late first century over the identity and future of Israel. Josephus wrote after 70 c.e., and this affects his descriptions of the Pharisees. We can be a bit more confident, therefore, in describing the historical Pharisees following the destruction of the Temple than explaining their origins or defining their role or place within Judaism in the early first century. Questions regarding the Pharisees at the time of Hillel and Jesus are of interest, but I think it is more relevant for interpreting Gospel texts to understand who the Pharisees were when the Gospel narratives were written.

These two definitions of the Pharisees converge on some significant points. Neusner and Rivkin agree that the sources indicate that the Pharisees were influential in both public and religious spheres after 70 c.e. Whatever their role within Judaism might have been prior to 70, the Pharisees emerged as the leading contenders for redefining Judaism in the wake of the destruction of the Temple. Other groups, named and unnamed, zealous advocates for the revolt against Rome, the Sadducees and other priests associated with the Temple, the sectarian Essenes, were eliminated or had no claim to leadership. The best-known group today that survived along with the Pharisees was a relatively small minority and quite new. The story of this group is told in the Gospels. The Pharisees succeeded in determining the future of Judaism, focusing on the interpretation of the divinely inspired Written and Oral Torah. The minority group took another path toward a different future, grounded in the acclamation of God's Messiah, Jesus of Nazareth. Their dominance came with Constantine's conversion in the fourth century and the establishment of Christianity as the religion of the Empire.

I think it is worth noting that Neusner's definition of the Pharisees, which Christians have readily appropriated, relates only to the time of Hillel and Jesus. In my opinion, the transformations of the Pharisees from political influence and popularity in the Hasmonean period to pietistic separatists in the early first century, and back to public and religious leadership after 70, represent dramatic shifts in identity and roles in a relatively short time. Notwithstanding the fluidity in the role of the Pharisees in Jewish life over more than two centuries, the move from separatists to leading contenders for both public and religious leadership within a few decades seems improbable. It is more likely that the Pharisees were popular religious leaders with a role in public affairs and that they were well positioned to survive and to redefine Jewish identity after the destruction of the Temple. Rivkin may be faulted for not giving more attention to the significance of the destruction of the Temple in altering the definition of the Pharisees, but I would argue for more continuity than discontinuity between the Pharisees before and after 70. So while we will focus our attention on the Pharisees at the time the Gospels were written, the Pharisees of Jesus' day were not very different. They were the respected interpreters of Oral Torah who made observance accessible to ordinary Jewish life.

The Oral Torah

What is the Oral Torah, or Oral Law? This is an important question because it involves the relationship between the Written Torah and the emergence of the authority of Oral Law alongside the Scriptures. It is crucial for Christian preachers because few have knowledge of the existence of Oral Torah and its significance for first-century Judaism, and because it affects our reading of the Gospels.

Quite simply, the Oral Torah consists of teachings and interpretations of traditions transmitted orally. The Oral Torah apparently originated and attained authoritative status alongside the Written Torah in the second century B.C.E., in the Maccabean period. The Oral Torah is closely associated with the Pharisees, and these teachings "embodied the social, cultural and religious traditions adhered to by a majority of Second Temple Jewry."[17] The Sadducees explicitly rejected the Oral Torah and regarded only the Written Torah (the first five books of the Scriptures, also called the Law of Moses) as authoritative for Jewish life and practice. The Oral Torah does not consist simply of interpretations of written texts. The relationship between Written Torah and Oral Torah is complex. A passage from the *Mishnah*, the first written codification of Oral Torah at the beginning of the third century C.E., puts it this way: The *halakhot* [laws] of release from vows hover in the air and have nothing to support them. The *halakhot* of Shabbat, of festival offering, and of sacrilege are as mountains hanging by a hair: scripture is scanty but the *halakhot* are many" (*Mishnah Hagigah* 1:8). In other words, sometimes the oral teaching interprets a biblical law, expanding and developing it in new contexts, as in the case of Sabbath observances. In other instances, the oral customs are independent of the Scriptures, as in the case of laws related to release from vows. And, of course, the oral traditions and the biblical laws are at other times closely related.

The Oral Torah was created and transmitted in a variety of public settings. Teachers taught small groups of students; they taught in assemblies, in the marketplace, in synagogue homilies, at communal meals.[18] There was no central legislative institution, no final arbitrator on correct observance, no established method of enforcement. The development of Oral Torah was organic, characterized by diversity and flexibility, the capacity for innovation, adaptability, and creativity. Obviously, when we take into account the Oral Torah as an aspect of the context for the Gospels, we will read controversies over the Law differently.

Other Views

Neusner and Rivkin are not the only scholars who have contributed to the study of the historical Pharisees. I use their work here because they were the first to do a comprehensive study of the primary sources and they serve as a model for a critical construction of the historical Pharisees. By comparing their studies, we learn of the complexities involved in defining the historical Pharisees.

One of the more recent significant and original contributions to the study of the Pharisees comes from Anthony Saldarini. In his book, *Pharisees, Scribes, and Sadducees in Palestinian Society*, he undertakes a social analysis of these Jewish groups in the Hasmonean and Herodean periods (that is, before the destruction of the Temple). Saldarini looks at these groups concentrating on "their communal activities and functions in society rather than on a static list of characteristics." He defines the Pharisees as a retainer class: "They were a literate, corporate, voluntary association which constantly sought influence with the governing class. As such they belonged to the retainer class, a group of people above the peasants and other lower classes but dependent on the governing class and ruler for their place in society." And, as such, their influence and power was never secure or stable like those groups defined by hereditary ties or traditional roles of leadership.[19]

Though Saldarini's study focuses on the Pharisees before the destruction of the Temple, there are several valuable insights relevant to the interpretation of the Gospels. First, the Pharisees were one group among many, named and unnamed. Christians schooled in the Gospels tend to overemphasize the Pharisees' power and importance, especially in the time of Jesus. Second, the Pharisees were a voluntary group. Members had different levels of involvement, they belonged to other groups, and they earned a living in a variety of ways. As a group and as individuals, the Pharisees had multiple functions in society. Third, the Pharisees were not a part of the governing class; they competed for influence and power. The Gospels do not give us any idea of the diverse functions of the Pharisees in society, and they imply greater power than is historically probable. Finally, though the Pharisees in Galilee differed from those in Jerusalem, they represented a faction that likely disagreed with Jesus and his followers over political and religious matters.[20] The prominent role of the Pharisees in the Gospels, especially in Matthew and Luke, relates to experiences in Judaism after 70, but the Pharisees were not absent from the pre-Gospel stories of Jesus. Again, while groups who survive the destruction of the Temple do not survive unchanged, there is some continuity in identity.

Positive Portrayals of the Pharisees in the Synoptic Gospels

The prevailing impression of the Pharisees in Matthew, Mark, and Luke is negative. They are the leading opponents of Jesus and the disciples, and they appear characteristically concerned with the minutiae of the Law and defenders of religious orthodoxy. But the Gospel portrayal of the Pharisees is not uniformly hostile. They are not always presented as enemies of Jesus and his followers. While the Pharisees typically function as antagonists, they often have a positive function in the Gospels. We tend to miss the more positive presentations because we are so conditioned to read with the stereotypes in mind, so much so that we sometimes read them into texts where they are absent.

The Pharisees, who are the primary adversaries in the controversies with Jesus during his ministry, are not named in the Passion narratives. In what is regarded as the earliest written narrative, preceding the composition of the Gospels, the named opponents are chief priests and scribes. What are we to make of the explicit absence of the Pharisees in the narrative of the betrayal, trial, and execution of Jesus? This might be a matter of historical reality. It is possible that those who constructed this early tradition knew that the Pharisees were not involved, did not have sufficient power or influence at the time of Jesus' death, or were particularly vulnerable in relationship to the Roman authorities. I think the absence of named Pharisees in the Passion narrative does lend credence to the argument that the Pharisees were introduced into controversy stories when the Gospels were written, around 70 C.E. and later. The Pharisees were the foremost rivals of the followers of Jesus after the destruction of the Temple and much less so before then. We can only speculate about the reason they are absent as a named group opposing Jesus. Preachers are advised to take note and not presume the Pharisees are present and culpable.

The portrayal of the Pharisees in the Synoptic Gospels is closely related to the subject of Torah observance.[21] We noted above that Mark devotes the least attention to Torah observance; here we observe that the Pharisees are less prominent in Mark than in Matthew or Luke. They are portrayed as antagonists of Jesus in three controversies (2:15-18; 2:23-28; 3:1-6) and, on one occasion, as allies of the Herodians who conspire to destroy Jesus (3:6). The strongest condemnation of the Pharisees appears in 7:1-13. They are called hypocrites and charged with abandoning the commandments of God for the sake of their own human tradition. There is a sharp criticism of the "tradition of the elders" (7:5), which is another name for the Oral Law.[22] The depiction of the Pharisees is hardly flattering in Mark, but the earliest Gospel lacks the intense polemic of Matthew and the more nuanced portrayal of Luke. (We will work with the two-source hypothesis here, positing the priority of Mark, Mark as a source for Luke and Matthew, Q as a source for Luke and Matthew, and no direct literary link between Luke and Matthew.)

The sharpest polemic against the Pharisees belongs to Matthew. The litany against the "scribes, Pharisees, hypocrites" in Matthew 23 is the harshest condemnation of the Pharisees found in the Gospels. A look at Gospel parallels reveals an intensification of criticisms against the Pharisees in Matthew's redaction of Mark and perhaps of Q as well. (It is difficult to assess redactions of Q; we cannot be sure whether Matthew or Luke or neither or both edited the Q source. Where Matthew and Luke rely on Q, criticism of the Pharisees is generally stronger in Matthew than in Luke.) Even in Matthew, though, the Pharisees are occasionally presented in a positive way. They are acknowledged as models of righteousness: "For I tell you, unless your righteousness exceeds that of the scribes and Pharisees, you will never enter the kingdom of heaven" (5:20). Righteousness implies Torah observance, according to Matthew, and the Pharisees set the standard for excellence. This is confirmed in Matt. 23:2-3a: "The scribes and Pharisees sit on Moses' seat; therefore, do whatever they teach you and follow it." The litany of hypocrisy follows, but the recognition of the Pharisees' role as interpreters of Oral and Written Torah and the admonition to follow their teachings is also present. (According to Pharisaic tradition, the Oral Torah was given to Moses at Sinai along with the Written Torah.)[23]

Matthew provides the substantive material for the Christian stereotype of the Pharisees. But the polemic may tell us more about the social situation of the author and audience of this Gospel than about the Pharisees. In an important article, "The New Testament's Anti-Jewish Slander and the Conventions of Ancient Polemic," Luke Timothy Johnson shows that this polemic must be understood within the social context of Hellenistic philosophical schools.[24] The slander found in the Newer Testament uses conventional language typically used by rival philosophical schools, including rival Jewish groups. He demonstrates that the conventional language is simply what opponents said about each other. "Blind guides" (23:16, 24) and "white-washed tombs" (23:27) belong to the stock invective of the ancient rhetoric. The slander against the Pharisees in the diatribe in Matthew 23 tells us only that the Pharisees were rivals of the Matthean community; it does not describe the historical Pharisees. Johnson also observes that the intensity of the polemic increased in relationship to a decreased sense of influence and power. This was likely the situation of the author and audience of Matthew in relationship to the Pharisees, and it is consistent with Matthew's acknowledging of the Pharisees' respected place as interpreters of Torah and at the same time regarding them as rivals for defining Jewish identity.

Luke presents the most favorable portrayal of the Pharisees. They play a prominent role in the narrative but without the persistent polemic we read in Matthew. The controversies are focused on issues, particularly Torah observance. There is no general condemnation of the Pharisees.[25] Furthermore, we see diversity among the Pharisees within Luke. The subtleties and complexity of the picture of the Pharisees in this Gospel require an extended discussion.

Luke's redaction of controversies shared with Mark and Matthew softens criticisms of the Pharisees. Pharisees first appear in Luke in the pericope on the healing of the paralytic lowered through the roof (5:17-26; parallels Mark 2:1-12; Matt. 9:1-8). Luke introduces the Pharisees into the narrative; they are absent in Mark. The Pharisees are present at the beginning, at the point of controversy, and at the end. They gather from "every village of Galilee and Judea and from Jerusalem" and sit nearby as Jesus is teaching (5:17). The Pharisees, along with the scribes, challenge Jesus for pronouncing forgiveness of sins for the paralytic. They question: "Who is this who is speaking blasphemies? Who can forgive sins but God alone?" (5:21). Jesus perceives their questioning (Luke omits the discussion of the questions among themselves found in Mark 2:8), and poses an unanswerable question as to whether it is easier to heal or to forgive sins. He heals the man, and, in Luke's conclusion to the pericope, "Amazement seized all of them, and they glorified God and were filled with awe, saying, 'We have seen strange things today'" (5:26). In Luke's version of the story, the Pharisees are present in the beginning as eager listeners who had traveled from many places to hear Jesus teach, and they are there at the end, implied by the "all" who were amazed and awed and who glorified God. The controversy is over the particular question of the authority to forgive sins, and, in this instance, Luke's Pharisees join the rest of the crowd in glorifying God.

In the two Sabbath observance controversies shared with Mark, Luke makes subtle changes that focus the conflict on legal differences. For example, in the controversy over plucking grain on the Sabbath, Luke adds that the disciples "rubbed [the heads of grain] in their hands, and ate them" (6:1). The act of grinding the grain heads and eating them narrows the focus to circumstances under which one may prepare food for consumption, which was the basis for legal debate. Jesus defends the action by appealing to Scripture. In the controversy over healing the man with a withered hand (6:6-11; Mark 3:1-6; Matt. 12:9-14), Luke adds that Jesus *taught* when he entered the synagogue, thus indicating that he was an insider customarily present (see also Luke 4:16). Luke adds that the man's *right* hand was withered (v. 6), perhaps implying that the handicap hindered the man's ability to work or inhibited social interactions. Luke's redaction names the Pharisees at the point of controversy, watching to see whether Jesus would cure the man. In contrast to Mark's "so that they might accuse him," Luke adds that they might "find an accusation against him" (Mark 3:2; Luke 6:7). In other words, simply healing the man would not necessarily be a breach of Sabbath law; there were many, many circumstances that allowed for healing on the Sabbath, so a case must still be made. Luke adds, too, that Jesus "knew what they were thinking" (v. 8). We ought not infer that Jesus had extraordinary perceptive power, nor that the Pharisees' thoughts were hostile. The author perhaps implies that Jesus was familiar with the Pharisees' reasoning on matters of observance.[26] In agreement with Mark, Luke's Jesus defends the healing by appealing to the rubric, "Is it lawful to do good or to do harm on the sabbath?" Luke omits Jesus' anger and grief at the opponents' hardness of heart (Mark 3:5). Mark names the Pharisees at the end of the pericope, conspiring with the Herodians to destroy Jesus. By comparison, Luke's conclusion is mild, indicating that "they" (the Pharisees are implied but not named) were furious and "discussed with one another what they might do to Jesus."

Luke includes two Sabbath controversies unique to this Gospel. One, the healing of a crippled woman, does not name the Pharisees but, given the synagogue setting and the issue of Sabbath observance, may imply their presence (13:10-17). On this occasion, Jesus defends the healing with a principle of legal interpretation, arguing from the lesser to the greater: you would *untie* an animal on the Sabbath to give it a drink, all the more would you *untie* a woman from her bondage. The narrative setting of the second Lukan Sabbath healing is a meal at the home of a leader of the Pharisees (14:1-6). When Jesus asks the lawyers and Pharisees present whether it is lawful to cure people on the Sabbath, they are silent. Their silence does not imply that it was unlawful; healing was permitted under many circumstances, and the tendency in interpretation was toward leniency. Jesus defends the healing of the man with dropsy by applying a hermeneutical principle similar to the one in 13:10-17.

Some knowledge of the Oral Torah concerning healing on the Sabbath enlightens our understanding of these Sabbath controversies in Luke. A common misperception is that healing was permitted on the Sabbath *only* in the most extreme circumstances, *only* when life was in danger. When this supposition is applied to these controversies, one inevitably concludes that the issue was Jesus' humanitarianism versus the inflexibility on the part of the Pharisees to bend the Law in the face of human need or suffering. But according to *Mishnah*, the rubric on Sabbath healing is "*whenever* there is *doubt whether* life is in danger, this overrides the Sabbath" (*Yoma* 8:6; italics mine). The discussion shows how very lenient was the interpretation of "doubt," including ravenous hunger, sore throat, and satisfying a pregnant woman's craving for food.[27]

Luke presents Jesus as being within the Law.[28] Jesus always justifies his action on the basis of the Law, typically citing a maxim on which all would agree, such as doing good on the Sabbath, or treating a person with the consideration one accords an animal. But that does not mean that all would have agreed with Jesus' interpretation or that the maxim fit the situation. In the Sabbath healings in Luke, Jesus heals individuals with birth defects and with chronic conditions, and theoretically such healing could have been postponed a few hours. On the one hand, the Gospel writer conveys a respect for Torah observance and Pharisaic methods of legal interpretation; on the other hand, he shows Jesus' authority to interpret the Law.

Luke distinguishes *among* the Pharisees. The author often qualifies references to the Pharisees, by adding "some." Only some of the Pharisees challenge the disciples in the grain field (6:2). The preface to the parable of the Pharisee and the tax collector identifies the audience as "some who trusted in themselves that they were righteous" (18:9). Some Pharisees befriend Jesus, warning him of Herod's intent to kill him (13:31).[29] And individual Pharisees extend to Jesus invitations for dinner (in addition to the Sabbath meals mentioned above, see also 7:36; 11:37). Some of the Pharisees are believers (Acts 15:5), indicating the permeable boundaries between these Jewish groups. The Pharisees who are not believers are consistently defenders of the believers, according to Acts. A Pharisee named Gamaliel, "a teacher of the law, respected by all the people" (5:34), defends the apostles before the Sanhedrin and allows them to continue to preach, lest the council be found "fighting against God!" (v. 39). The Pharisees defend Paul before the Sanhedrin (23:6-9), finding nothing about him that is objectionable. Paul in Acts is the perfect Torah-observant Pharisee. The Pharisees are never opponents of the believers in Acts.

The Pharisees in Luke grumble and complain that Jesus eats with tax collectors and sinners (5:30; 15:2). In response, Jesus both admonishes and affirms them. At the banquet at Levi the tax collector's home, Jesus directs his response to the Pharisees' complaints to his disciples, "Those who are well have no need of a physician, but those who are sick; I have come to call not the righteous but sinners to repentance" (5:31-32; note that Luke adds "to repentance"). Tax collectors and sinners, Pharisees and scribes comprise the narrative audience for three related parables unique to Luke (15:1-32). Jesus responds to the grumbling by telling three parables that make the same point, namely, there is joy in heaven over the return of one repentant sinner. Luke's Jesus thus reminds the Pharisees that in the kingdom of God there is room at the table, now and proleptically at the heavenly banquet table, for even the most conspicuous sinner who repents. At the same time, the conclusion of the first parable acknowledges the "ninety-nine righteous persons who need no repentance" (v. 7). Likewise, at the conclusion of the third parable, the parable of the two brothers (in Christian tradition called "The Prodigal Son"), the father assures the elder brother, "Son, you are always with me, and all that is mine is yours" (v. 31). Given the narrative setting of these parables, a first-century audience easily would have made the connection between the listening tax collectors and sinners and the repentant sinners in the parables; and I submit they would also have recognized the listening Pharisees as the righteous ones in the parables, including the elder brother for whom the promises of God are assured. Luke's Jesus chides the Pharisees to make room at the table for the most marginalized repentant sinners; Jesus also here confirms their righteousness, expressed in Torah observance, and assures their place at the table.

The Pharisees are also portrayed as rivals. We find in Luke the same conventional language of ancient polemic that we see in Matthew, most of which comes from the shared Q source. The denunciations of the Pharisees are concentrated in Luke 11:37-54. The passage begins with an invitation to dinner, so the polemic occurs at the table. At the conclusion, the Pharisees "began to be very hostile toward him and to cross-examine him about many things." Luke describes the Pharisees as "lovers of money" (16:14), another charge common in the polemical rhetoric of rival philosophical schools.[30]

Many conflicts with the Pharisees occur at the table, not an insignificant aspect of Luke's narrative. Table fellowship is a key theme in Luke-Acts, motivated in part, I believe, by the real issues in the nascent Christian communities over table fellowship. Such fellowship could include people with different customs and traditions, very observant Pharisees, Jews indifferent to matters of observance, and non-Jews, around the same table. Sharing a meal, ritual or otherwise, is a family or communal affair. Placing the controversies with Pharisees at the table implies that the debates are within the family, certainly within Judaism, likely intra-Pharisaic, and suggestive of issues within the communities of believers.

Overall, the Pharisees have a positive function in Luke and its sequel, the Acts of the Apostles. Even in the controversies, they have a positive role; as Robert Brawley observes, "Luke's Jesus will make slight impression on his readers if his antagonists are opponents of straw." And the conflicts frequently have an "insider's" character. The distinctions among the Pharisees temper any inference of general hostility. The author expects the audience to resonate positively with the Pharisees as the respected leaders of Judaism.[31] Contemporary Christian audiences must overcome a long history of a caricature of the Pharisees and negative constructions of Judaism to hear it.

The Synoptic Gospel authors depict the Pharisees in light of their experiences with them in the formative years of Jewish self-definition in the late first century. The purpose of the Gospels is not to provide an objective definition of the historical Pharisees. The Gospels portray the Pharisees in accordance with the literary conventions of late antiquity. When encountering the Pharisees in the Gospel stories, preachers might pay less attention to *what* is said than *how* it is said and to consider individual pericopes within the whole narrative. Recognizing the more positive pictures of the Pharisees provides a helpful corrective to the prevailing perception that the Pharisees were consistently hostile opponents of Jesus and the early believers.

Misrepresentations and Correctives in Preaching

There are some frequent and familiar ways that caricatures of the Pharisees and the Law occur in sermons. The purpose here is to identify them and suggest some ways that preachers can both avoid the stereotypes *and* offer a more accurate presentation, based on reliable historical sources and consideration of the Gospels in their late first-century context. It is not enough to recognize and to resist relying on negative portrayals in a homily. When the Pharisees are present in the biblical text, Christian listeners usually identify them in terms of the long history of contempt. Mary Boys sums up the problem this way: "If, however, the conventional account of Christian origins still rings in our ears, it is very difficult to hear the deeper resonances of texts about the Pharisees. . . . The conventional account works on the equation, 'self-righteous Pharisees equals legalistic Judaism.' It thereby obscures the complexity of life in the early church by reducing the conflict to Jesus versus Judaism."[32] The preacher's task is to challenge the conventional account.

The most common presentation of the Pharisees and the Law in preaching is as a foil, to emphasize the superiority of Jesus and Christianity. Again, this is not surprising, since this is how the Pharisees and other representatives of the Jewish leadership often function in the text. The busy preacher is vulnerable too, because the text tends to lead one to exaggerate the negative images, and because homiletical resources and commentaries typically reinforce the tendency. For example, a contributor to *The Living Pulpit* used the Pharisees to justify an instance of Jesus' intolerance:

> Many of the rules and regulations created by the scribes and Pharisees created systemic injustices. They artificially and unnecessarily burdened believers. Jesus simply could not remain silent in the face of such an intolerable misuse of religion. He refused to tolerate the intolerable.[33]

This is a good example of the prevalence of this caricature of the Pharisees, so much so that it functions as a foil apart from the exegesis of any particular text. This is simply presented as who the Pharisees were.

The Pharisees need not appear in a text for them to function as a foil. In a sermon on Mark 10:17, the story of the rich young man who asks Jesus what he must do to inherit eternal life, the Pharisees serve as a contrast to the sincere inquirer, though they are not mentioned in the pericope:

> *He did not come to Jesus with verbal puzzles, mental gymnastics, and pious theological jargon. That was what the Pharisees did. They would come before him and say: 'Jesus, what do you think about paying taxes to Caesar? Jesus what do you think about divorce? Jesus, what do you think about an afterlife? Why don't your disciples fast? Wash their hands? Obey the Sabbath?' The fact is that they could care less* [sic] *what he thought about any of those things. They were asking him these questions simply to trip him up and make him commit that one fatal verbal error that might hang him. They were arrogant. But this man ran to Jesus, knelt before him in the middle of the road. And asked sincere questions.*[34]

This characterization of the Pharisees goes beyond a literal reading of the Gospel stories to magnify their faults and devious intent.

The most disturbing and frankly offensive portrayal I have found of the Pharisees as a foil casts them as the model of "chronic anxiety" described in Rabbi Edwin Friedman's family-systems theory. According to the sermon, the Pharisees demonstrate chronic anxiety when they warn Jesus to flee, that Herod wants to kill him (Luke 13:31-35):

The Pharisees lived in chronic anxiety fearful of the cultural accommodations Jews were making to Gentile ways, believing Torah offered the quick fix to keep the faith alive, fostering polarizations along the lines of Jew and Gentile, clean and unclean, sinner and righteous. Theirs was a world of labels and categories and rules. It was how they sought order in their chaotic world. They failed to see their own role in the chaos and anxiety of their times. . . . So here come the Pharisees to warn Jesus that Herod is out to get him. Anxious people love to create more anxiety.[35]

The sermon later cites Rabbi Friedman's observation that "there is no way out of a chronic [anxiety] condition unless one is willing to go through an acute, temporarily more painful, phase." The preacher then attributes to Friedman a meaning he certainly does not intend: "That sounds like a Jewish rabbi talking about the cross to me."[36] This description of the Pharisees has little support in the Gospels, none in the Gospel text that purportedly provides the basis for the sermon, and bears no relationship to the historical Pharisees. It belittles the Judaism of Jesus' day and Rabbi Friedman's own Jewish faith by defining his observation about the chronically anxious system in Christian terms. And, the sermon misses an opportunity to underscore the positive portrayal of the Pharisees in this Lukan passage.

An interpreter must first develop awareness of how the presentation of the Pharisees reinforces Christian stereotypes of Judaism. In a typical controversy story, for example (Mark 2:23-28; parallels in Matt. 12:1-8 and Luke 6:1-5), the Pharisees question Jesus when they see his disciples plucking heads of grain in the grain fields, "Look, why are they doing what is not lawful on the sabbath?" The pericope concludes with Jesus' pronouncement, "The sabbath was made for humankind, and not humankind for the sabbath," and the narrator's summary, "So the Son of Man is lord even of the sabbath." The temptation here is to exaggerate the Pharisaic obsession with the Law, placing it above consideration for human needs, in contrast to Jesus' compassion and supposed disregard for meaningless observances. And Christian ears will likely hear that contrast when the Gospel is read. As a corrective, a preacher might make a few positive remarks about Torah observance and the importance of Sabbath observances in early Judaism. One might place the debate over Sabbath observance within the context of late first-century Judaism.

The text indicates the importance of Sabbath observance in Jesus' response to the Pharisees' question. He defends the disciples by citing Scripture and a common maxim concerning the Sabbath. "The sabbath was made for humankind, not humankind for the sabbath" is not original with Jesus; it reflects general wisdom concerning the sabbath. The narrator's conclusion, that Jesus is lord "*even* of the sabbath," confirms the relevance of Sabbath observance from the perspective of the Gospel writer, as well as the conviction that Jesus is the authoritative interpreter of Sabbath customs. Regardless of the sermon's theme for the occasion, in a few sentences the preacher can reframe the controversy to address common assumptions of Pharisaic legalism and Jesus' rejection of the Law.

Barbara K. Lundblad's sermon on the call of Matthew the tax collector and the dinner at his home (Matt. 9:9-13) provides a good example for handling texts containing controversies with the Pharisees:

> *Now we need to be careful with stories like this one. It is far too easy for those of us who are Christians to scold the Pharisees for being judgmental, snobbish, rude—and cowardly! After all, they didn't even dare to go directly to Jesus with their complaint to the disciples: "Why does your teacher eat with tax collectors and sinners?" It's important to remember that probably everyone in this story is Jewish: Jesus, his disciples, the tax collectors, at least some of the sinners, and the Pharisees. This gospel was written many years after Jesus' life, death and resurrection. Tensions broke out between Jews and those who came to be called "Christians." These tensions seep back into the gospel stories and we are always in danger of painting "the Jews" as the problem. Now this isn't only the tragedy of anti-Semitism; it's also an attitude which distances. It's about those nasty Pharisees—not me.*[37]

In just a few sentences she contextualizes the pericope within Judaism, reflecting late first-century controversies, and she identifies the problem as not only anti-Semitism but our missing what the Scriptures say to us.

Another strategy for minimizing anti-Jewish tendencies in controversy texts is to highlight points of agreement. For example, in the Synoptic Gospels the Sabbath controversies imply that Sabbath customs matter to the authors and audiences. Jesus is presented within the Law, not against it. The issue is the claim for Jesus' authority to interpret the Law. In a sermon on the healing of the paralytic (Mark 2:1-12), I identified the implied agreement between Jesus and the scribes:

The scribes understood perfectly the implication of Jesus' words, "Your sins are forgiven." Jesus was claiming divine authority. Only God can forgive sins. Jesus and the scribes are on the same page. It takes no great power of perception on Jesus' part to know what the scribes were thinking. He is announcing for all to hear that the boundary between heaven and earth has been crossed.[38]

I continued by inviting us to consider the scribes' experience as similar to our own when we are challenged to rethink our cherished ideas:

The scribes get it; so do we. We know what it is like when we are pushed to rethink our own perceptions of reality, of God's place in our ordered world, who we understand God to be, and how we relate to God. The scribes question in their hearts what is at stake if Jesus' claim to authority is for real. Good question. The boundaries constructed to protect their/our comfort zone and to contain God are no longer secure.[39]

The theme of the sermon was the God who breaks our carefully constructed boundaries. I tried to present a sympathetic picture of the scribes by connecting them experientially with the listeners so that it would be very difficult to dismiss them as mere antagonists of Jesus. And I noted that the scribes—and us!—are included in all who were amazed and glorified God (v. 12).

Some texts are more explicit about points of agreement. In the preface to the parable of the Good Samaritan, the lawyer gives the answer to his own question, "What must I do to inherit eternal life?" And Jesus agrees with his answer, citing from Deuteronomy and Leviticus (Luke 10:25-28). He also answers Jesus' question as to who was a neighbor in the parable. "The one who showed him mercy," the lawyer answered (v. 28). And Jesus agrees with him. Drawing attention to the accord between the lawyer and Jesus provides a corrective to the inclination to create sharp contrasts at the expense of the lawyer. Further, one need not be overly disparaging of the priest and the Levite in the parable; the parable works because they were from respected Jewish groups.

In the Synoptic Gospels, the scribes and lawyers frequently appear in the same role as the Pharisees, that is, as antagonists to Jesus and the disciples, and in Christian tradition they all represent deficiencies in Judaism. These groups were not identical in the first century. The scribes were not "a coherent social group with a set membership, but rather a class of literate individuals drawn from many parts of society who filled various social roles and were attached to all parts of society from the village to the palace and Temple." They were not an autonomous group.[40] They may have been more closely associated with the Pharisees following the destruction of the Temple; they and the Pharisees are often mentioned together in the Gospels. Lawyers were simply experts in legal matters; they were not a formal group. I think the Gospel authors knew the differences among the groups and were intentional in naming them. For instance, in the healing of the paralytic, Luke's version introduces Pharisees where the Markan source names scribes (Luke 5:17-26). I suggest that preachers follow the text in identifying representatives of competing Jewish groups. Where the text names scribes, do not call them Pharisees. To do so reinforces the "Pharisees equals legalistic Judaism" equation.

When we encounter ridicule or general condemnation in the Gospel narratives, there is a predisposition toward literalism on the part of both preachers and listeners. We are conditioned to hear the harsh judgments as justified. If Jesus says the Pharisees are hypocrites, then they must have been hypocrites. Would he call them "lovers of money" if it were not true? Depending on circumstances, the sermon may or may not be the appropriate place to say that Jesus most likely did not say these things or that the polemic against the Pharisees corresponds to the context of the Gospel communities. I do occasionally refer to "Mark's Jesus," or "Jesus according to Luke," as a way to circumvent literalism. One can point out the use of hyperbole and place the polemical name-calling within its *literary* context, as part of the rhetoric of competing groups. In a recent homily, I handled one of these passages this way:

Now, Matthew's Jesus has some harsh words for the Pharisees here. We don't know if Jesus resorted to name-calling, but we do recognize hyperbole when we hear it. And this kind of polemical language was common among competing groups in the first century, including different Jewish groups. These names are just what they called each other. Maybe directly to their face. Maybe not. It was what they wrote about each other. The Pharisees were no more hypocritical than any other group. They were actually very respected by most people, including among the followers of Jesus.[41]

When the Pharisees appear as a foil in the Gospels, I am tempted to do too much explaining to try to solve the problem in one sermon. I believe that a few sentences designed to challenge the negative images of Christian tradition is more effective and a more realistic goal for preaching.

Ritual Purity Laws

Christian interpreters typically regard the ritual purity laws with the same antipathy as they do the Pharisees. Few understand these observances, and because these customs are so far removed from modern experience it is very easy to resort to a caricature of this aspect of Jewish life presuming that Jesus rejected these customs. I heard a sermon based on Mark 7 in which the preacher belittled the Pharisees for being so dense, for thinking rules about cleanliness came from God, and not knowing that what you do from the heart defiles, not what you eat. He concluded with a "Well, duh" to emphasize their obtuseness concerning such meaningless minutia.

A sermon entitled "Getting Down and Dirty" exemplifies common Christian prejudices about ritual purity laws. The preacher asserts that these laws were "the essence of Jewish religious practice during the time of Jesus."[42] He describes these laws and their origin:

> But about 400–500 years before Jesus' birth, a class of religious legal experts called the Scribes came about. They expanded and amplified these principles until there were literally thousands of little rules and regulations governing nearly every situation in life. This comprised the Oral Law *which came to be written down about three centuries after Jesus' death. That written summary is the* Mishnah. *The effect of centuries of tradition and interpretation was that ethical religion became buried under a huge mass of taboos and rules.*[43]

Beyond the disparity between Jewish ritual law and ethics, there are several historical inaccuracies: the scribes were not legal experts predating Jesus by centuries, they did not develop the Oral Law, the *Mishnah* is much more than a written summary of purity laws, and, of course, they were not the essence of Judaism, an assertion that occurs more than once in this sermon on Mark 7.

Several years ago I assigned in my classes an exegetical paper on the story of the hemorrhaging woman, Mark 5:21-43. I have since changed the pericope for the assignment, because the resulting exegesis of the narrative was disturbingly predictable. Students asserted that the woman was in a constant state of impurity and therefore a social outcast because of her twelve-year flow of blood. No one dared touch her or even come near her for fear of becoming unclean. Jesus, however, responded to her touch by healing her, thus showing compassion where the laws did not allow for it. Observations about the sexism of laws that affected women adversely, presumably laws that Jesus clearly dismissed, were also common. In fairness to the students, they documented respected sources for their reading of the pericope.

In the first place, the text gives no indication that purity observances are at issue here. There is no indication that anyone avoided her. She is in the midst of a crowd pressing around Jesus, so that Jesus does not know who touched him. Her plight is due to a medical condition. We read that "she had endured much under many physicians, and had spent all that she had; and she was no better, but rather grew worse" (v. 26). That is why she sought healing from Jesus. Second, if the issue were related to ritual impurity, it does not follow that all avoided her for fear of becoming unclean. In fact, according to the narrative, no one in the crowd seemed aware that they may be contacting impurity from this woman.

Contacting ritual impurity was simply part of life for Jews in the ancient world. Systems defining ritual impurities were commonplace, not unique to Jews, though particulars and articulated meanings differed. There were many ways to contact impurity and there were prescribed rituals for removing an impurity. One could not possibly avoid all ritual impurities. E. P. Sanders observes that "All Jews, including Pharisees, were impure more or less all the time."[44] Ritual impurity is not synonymous with poor hygiene habits or uncleanness as we think of it. For example, according to *Mishnah*, "all the holy scriptures render the hands unclean."[45] The rabbis certainly did not refrain from contact with the Scriptures for fear of getting their hands dirty.

The rabbinic literature does describe a very detailed and complex system of ritual purity laws, containing some first-century observances along with later traditions. But the *Mishnah* conveys an ideal in ancient Judaism more than a manual for daily living.[46] It contains rabbinic legal arguments that are often hypothetical and reflects a system of thought that does not mirror the ambiguities of daily living. This does not mean that the customs were irrelevant or that observance was casual, but the practicalities of lived experience were more varied and complex than we typically imagine when we reconstruct reality on the basis of ancient texts. We draw false conclusions when we read them as a literal description of life in the ancient world.

Christian interpreters do not need to be fluent in the intricacies of ritual purity laws to avoid using them as a foil to display Jesus' superiority. We do need to remember that these laws, which seem to us strange and archaic, were not uncommon in the ancient world. It is anachronistic to suppose that Jesus dismissed them as irrelevant. Undoubtedly there was diversity with respect to attention to observance, some were more meticulous than others, and certainly there were differences in Diaspora customs. And we need to disconnect ritual impurity or ritual uncleanness from our modern concept of unclean as dirty or undesirable. This is probably the most common mistake biblical interpreters make. These laws were part of religious ritual. Perhaps part of the problem is that "ritual" has negative connotations for many Christians, implying a formal religious custom void of meaning, as in the sermon "Getting Down and Dirty" cited above. In the Gospel texts the criticism of ritual impurity laws relates to motives for observing laws, and we know that the charge for wrong motives is one for which there can be neither verification nor defense.

The Pharisees as a Mirror

A colleague at a neighboring seminary admonished his students, "Don't fall into the trap of painting the Pharisees as hypocritical cartoon characters. If you want to see what a Pharisee would look like today, look to your left and look to your right. They are us."[47] This is definitely a helpful hermeneutical approach. Rather than using them as a foil, the Pharisees become a mirror on our own behavior as Christians.

Several years ago, a seminary classmate told me about a sermon he had given in which he began by proclaiming to the congregation, "You are Pharisees!" He reported that they didn't appreciate it, though he did get their attention. His purpose, of course, was to move away from condemning the historical Pharisees and show that some of the things for which Jesus criticized the Pharisees he would also find troubling among upstanding Christians today. In a sermon given at Westminster Presbyterian Church in Minneapolis, Tim Hart-Anderson likened the behavior Jesus criticized in the Pharisees to our own: "We tend to want God to do our bidding, to fit into our box, to be limited to our own imagination. We want God to play by our rules."[48]

Barbara Brown Taylor's sermon on the familiar parable of the prodigal son (Luke 15:1-3, 11-32) describes a ministerial association offended by Jesus' dining companions in a restaurant. She identifies the ministerial association with the Pharisees who grumble and complain that Jesus eats with tax collectors and sinners (Luke 15:1-3).[49] This is very effective in making us see and feel ourselves reacting just like the Pharisees who were offended by the ones with whom Jesus chose to share a meal. She presented the Pharisees as good people, like us, but who are careful to keep the right company and steer clear of undesirables.[50]

The presentation of the Pharisees as a mirror on our own religious behavior has merit. Mary Boys sums it up nicely:

> The Pharisees function as mirrors, so those of us who take religious commitments seriously should turn the light of Jesus' critique of the Pharisees on ourselves. Who and what shocks us, and why? On what basis do we judge others, and what do our judgments reveal about our image of God? Does the wideness of God's mercy threaten us, call into question some of the narrowness of our own categories?[51]

This is a significant improvement over using the Pharisees as a foil and identifying our own religious disposition with Jesus. It goes far toward addressing the problem of defining Christianity over against inferior Judaism represented by the Pharisees.

I asked a preacher who is very intentional in addressing anti-Judaism in preaching, in teaching, and in liturgy how he handled the matter of the Pharisees in sermons. He said that he took a metaphorical approach. He pointed out that according to Jewish tradition, each person has within an inclination toward good (*yetzer ha-tov*) and an inclination toward evil (*yetzer ha-ra'*). I asked, "Do the Pharisees ever represent the *yetzer ha-tov*?"

When we limit the role of the Pharisees to exposing our shortcomings as religious persons we continue to cast them as flawed, in need of correction, and thereby lend justification to the Gospels' criticisms. I propose that we consider how the Pharisees represent our admirable qualities, at least occasionally. Granted, the Gospel texts do not lend themselves easily to such contemplation. But if we take seriously the historical context of the Gospels within the process of late first-century Jewish self-definition, we can imagine the controversies in light of faithful discernment of where God is leading Israel before the resolution of things we take for granted, before matters concerning Torah observances were settled, before there was Christianity separate from Judaism. If we allow a reliable historical definition of the Pharisees to challenge the long-standing stereotypes, then we can imagine them embodying the best of our religious inclinations.

The Pharisees were an innovative reform movement before the destruction of the Temple, and following 70 C.E. they succeeded in redefining Judaism in a radically changed historical context. In our own times, we might contend that we are at our best when we emulate them, reinterpreting the Scriptures and reimagining our faith in an ever-changing world. The Pharisees also claimed continuity with tradition, particularly related to Torah observance, and they appear as defenders of this divine revelation. At times we, like them, are at our best when we defend the traditions of our faith.

In a recent sermon on Mark 7, I featured the Pharisees more extensively than usual. The recent Episcopal General Convention's confirmation of an openly gay bishop provided the impetus, along with the lectionary Gospel for the day. In the congregation I serve most supported the convention's decision, and the few who did not were quiet about their objections. I followed the lead of our Presiding Bishop and Diocesan Bishop in advocating that we continue conversations with each other, and that we not allow this issue to divide us. The Pharisees provided a good model for diversity and the ability to hold in tension different views. A few excerpts from the sermon demonstrate how I offered the Pharisees as a positive example for us.

I began by identifying some favorite themes in this Gospel text: the Pharisees and the Judaism the Gospel writers knew, the tension between tradition and innovation, matters of revelation, and questions of identity. Then I gave a brief definition of the Pharisees:

I once delivered a lecture called: "Who were the Pharisees and why are they saying such terrible things about them?" In my reading and research, I discovered that the historical Pharisees were quite different than the polemic against them in the Newer Testament suggests. They were interpreters of tradition, of Scripture, interested in adapting religious observance to contemporary situations. And, they were creative and innovative in their interpretation of Scripture. They developed the Oral Torah. Mark refers to the "tradition of the elders" (7:3), which in other Jewish literature of the time is a formal synonym for Oral Torah, or Oral Law. (These laws were not committed to writing until much later.) These laws were like customs, fluid, flexible, adaptable, contextual, part of ongoing interpretation. And the Pharisees among themselves differed on interpretation, from very conservative to very liberal.

When I first discovered the Episcopal Church seventeen years ago, I said, "Wow! Episcopalians are a lot like the Pharisees!" A greater compliment I couldn't give. Committed to historic faith and to interpreting and living out that faith in light of cultural changes. Slow to change, yet believing that God continues to reveal God's self in the world around us. Holding that the truth revealed in the Scriptures must be always interpreted in light of tradition and reason and experience. And able to hold a wide range of beliefs and practices in our church without breaking communion. That's a good description of the character of the Episcopal Church—and of the Pharisees, too.

Okay, you're skeptical. If she's right about the Pharisees, then why do they come across in such a negative way in the Gospels? Why does Jesus, in Mark, condemn them? This is a family argument, within the family of Judaism, and there are disagreements. It is an easy charge to make, that the Pharisees hold to tradition without caring about spiritual matters or human needs, of placing human wisdom over God's truth. But if we could construct the Pharisaic argument here, the missing voices, we might hear that Torah, including the distinctive observances of Jews, are given by God, according to tradition given to Moses at Sinai. If we abandon them we are turning away from God. God entrusts humans to interpret them for new generations of Jews. If we abandon this tradition, we cut ourselves off from the traditions of our faith.

Tradition! A core aspect of our identity at St. Clement's is that we are traditional. Faithful to the Book of Common Prayer. Classical in our liturgy, in our choice of hymns and music. Attentive to the care and preservation of our historic building. But many Episcopalians would not regard St. Clement's as traditional at all. Many regard our general support—and that of our Diocese—for the consecration of bishop-elect Gene Robinson as a break from the traditional teachings of our church. From their point of view, this departs from the teachings of Scripture, represents reliance on human wisdom, places the whims of culture over God's laws on marriage and family. In their estimation we have abandoned tradition and the authority of the Scriptures.

What is tradition? What does it mean to preserve tradition? How do we put religious traditions into conversation with contemporary society, with the best of human wisdom, with new generations of the faithful? Faithful people answer differently.

Both the Pharisees and the early followers of Jesus, represented in Mark's Gospel, grounded their views in Scripture. The early believers made their case for the identity of Jesus on the basis of Scriptures; the Pharisees, too, were grounded in Scriptures, in the observance of Torah and its ongoing interpretation. Finally, for those who became known as Christians, the claim for Jesus as God's Messiah defined identity. For the Pharisees, and for succeeding Rabbinic Judaism, the tradition of observing Torah continued as a defining way of life. The result, finally in the second century, was schism. Two distinct identities. We take that schism as so inevitable that we read it back into the time of Jesus. This is an anachronism that causes us to miss so much of the texture and richness of our Christian beginnings, and so much of what our Scriptures have to teach us. And, of course, this has had horrific consequences for Jews living in the Western world dominated by Christianity.

I continued with a brief discussion of the current threat of schism in the Episcopal Church, expressing the hope that this issue not divide us, that we would respect each other in our differences and continue the conversation. I concluded with a return to the Pharisees:

> *One of my favorite things I learned about the Pharisees in reading their discussions of the Law is that they very often do not say what the final decision was. A debate on a particular law concludes: Rabbi so and so says this. And Rabbi so and so says this. They disagree. So, what's the verdict? Who won? Two opinions. No winners. No losers. Implied in these debates, I think, is the acknowledgment that God's truth has not yet been fully revealed. Meanwhile, we'll continue to talk with each other.*
>
> *I like that. That's a tradition I want to preserve at any cost.*[52]

While the feedback on the sermon was quite positive, one respondent criticized me for not preaching what the text says and for missing the perfect opportunity to speak a prophetic voice in support of full participation of gays and lesbians in the church. The point was well taken. But context informs the prophetic word, and on this occasion, I believed the prophetic word lay not in the validation of our own assessment of God's truth but in the challenge to resist disparaging those who did not agree. I think, too, that the prophetic word in our own time includes the refusal to use the Pharisees as a foil, aligning them with those whose religious views we oppose. And, there are many ways to preach the text!

Summary

Caricatures of the Pharisees and the rejection of the Law are key features of Christian anti-Judaism in sermons. In this chapter I maintain that knowledge of the historical Pharisees based on primary sources will help the preacher avoid the perpetuation of common stereotypes. Contrary to Christian tradition, the Pharisees were a popular group in the first century credited with the development of Oral Torah, unwritten laws that effectively made Torah observance widely accessible to Jews. They were one of many groups within early Judaism, and their influence and power varied throughout their history. In the late first century they emerged as leaders in defining Judaism after the destruction of the Temple in 70 c.e. While the primary sources do not support certainty in defining the Pharisees, there is sufficient evidence to contradict Christian suppositions that the Pharisees isolated themselves from others, that they had sufficient power to burden others with their laws, or that they advocated an inflexible legalism.

I also maintain that placing the Gospels within the context of late first-century Judaism provides an interpretive reference for preachers to address biases against the Pharisees and the Law. The Pharisees in the Synoptic Gospels relate primarily to the time of the Gospel authors and their communities in which the Pharisees were the primary contenders for defining the future of Judaism. The Gospels present the Pharisees as both respected leaders and opponents. The polemic against them indicates that they are opponents; it does not describe them as they were historically. Legal controversies are not a rejection of the Law but rather a confirmation of the importance of Torah observance within Judaism. Keeping in mind that the Gospels were, when they were written, Jewish literature and thus a part of intra-Jewish controversies, will help the preacher withstand the inclination to repeat anti-Jewish themes.

Popular preacher Barbara Brown Taylor wrote of a transformation in her own sermons with respect to Judaism:

> I look at sermons I wrote 15 years ago and I cannot believe some of the things I said about Pharisees, or about Judaism in general. My news source was the New Testament, which I accepted as the whole truth about "the Jews." Since then I have added enough Jewish news sources to my information bank to hear the gospel broadcast of the New Testament with far more attentive ears.[53]

My purpose in this chapter has been to add news sources to our information bank so that we do not unthinkingly resort to false and harmful stereotypes, and so that we and those who listen to our sermons hear the gospel of our Scriptures for our own lives.

4

The Gospel of John

THE GOSPEL OF JOHN differs from the Synoptic Gospels in several ways. Literary interdependence, common sources, and similar perspectives on the ministry of Jesus connect Matthew, Mark, and Luke and distinguish them from John. When we preach from John, we leave the more familiar world of the Synoptics and encounter the preexistent Logos, highly symbolic language, and lengthy, complex narratives. Jesus, according to John, does not teach in parables but in long discourses. His ministry of three years revolves around journeys in and out of Jerusalem; it is not located primarily in Galilee with a single journey to Jerusalem. Jesus' last meal with his disciples occurs on the day before Passover; it is not a Passover seder. These are just a few dissimilarities between John and the Synoptic Gospels, and they caution us against carrying our assumptions about Jesus' life and ministry to our reading of John without considering the distinctive characteristics of the Fourth Gospel. For our purposes here, however, the most significant characteristic of John is the sharpened polemic against "the Jews." Matthew, Mark, and Luke depict controversies with named Jewish groups, scribes, Pharisees, chief priests. In John, the opponents of Jesus and his followers are most often simply "the Jews."

The persistent portrayal of "the Jews" as adversaries presents a challenge for the preacher who is sensitive to the problem of Christian anti-Judaism. When asked for advice as to how to handle the problem of the hostility toward the Jews in the Fourth Gospel, John Dominic Crossan replied that we might have to refrain from public reading of this Gospel for a thousand years.[1] Barbara Brown Taylor admits: "There are whole chapters of John's Gospel that I would like to snip right out of the book so that no child ever has to read what John said Jesus said about Jews."[2] These are not realistic solutions to our difficulties with John, of course. They simply serve to under-score the very real problem we face in reading and interpreting John in the context of Christian worship these days. Taylor follows her acknowledged discomfort with these passages in John by observing that, "as long as Bibles keep coming out with those passages in them, then I have a responsibility to address them, if only to explain how they ever became part of the story in the first place."[3]

Is the Gospel of John Anti-Jewish?

Was the author of the Fourth Gospel anti-Jewish? That may seem like a rhetorical question, with the obvious answer in the affirma-tive. How else could one read the antagonism between the Jews and Jesus and his followers? According to John, Jesus asserts that the Jews are of the devil (8:44); the Jews threaten to stone Jesus (8:59; 10:33). The Jews (the crowds, or chief priests and scribes, according to the Synoptic Gospels) demand Jesus' death, ask for the release of Barabbas, and profess loyalty to the emperor 18:28—19:16). After Jesus' death, the disciples lock the doors "for fear of the Jews" (20:19). The most common reading of John is that the polemic against the Jews reflects the anti-Jewish sentiments of its author and commu-nity toward the end of the first century, separated from Judaism. But there are many scholars who place the Johannine community within the context of Judaism late in the first century. They define the polemic in John as part of an intra-Jewish conflict and, there-fore, not Christian anti-Judaism. So the question is a real one: Is this Gospel anti-Jewish? How we answer that question depends on (1) how we understand the term *Ioudaioi*; (2) how we understand the expulsion of community members from the synagogue; and (3) how we read the evidence of sectarianism in John.

Ioudaioi

Who were "the Jews" according to John? The term *Ioudaioi* in its singular and plural forms appears seventy-one times in the Gospel of John, much more frequently than in any of the other Gospels. Whereas the Synoptic Gospels name specific Jewish groups, Phari-sees, Sadducees, chief priests, and scribes, John characteristically refers to the Jews. Our ears hear "the Jews" in terms of how things turned out, in light of the separation between Judaism and Christianity and the long history of Jews as those who opposed Jesus and rejected Christianity. But in the first-century Greco-Roman world, *Ioudaioi* did not have the connotations we associate with Jews.

Within the Fourth Gospel, *Ioudaioi* does not always have the same meaning. It sometimes refers to people of Judea, sometimes to religious authorities, sometimes to a religious political group. For example, in 7:1-18, *Ioudaioi* seems to refer to Judeans, or a group located in Judea, as Jesus remained in Galilee because of the *Ioudaioi* in Judea. In 9:22, the *Ioudaioi* represent a subgroup of Judaism, specifically the synagogue leadership, or a faction within the synagogue. The parents of the blind man belong to the synagogue and fear the *Ioudaioi*. Religious authorities believed in Jesus but did not confess it because they feared expulsion from the synagogue (12:42). Others who are followers or friends of Jesus are Jews, by our definition, like Nicodemus the Pharisee (3:1; 7:50-51; 19:39) and Joseph of Arimathea (19:38), a secret believer for fear of the *Ioudaioi*. The *Ioudaioi* who come to comfort Mary and Martha when Lazarus dies are certainly good friends (11:31, 33) and many of them become believers (11:45). *Ioudaioi* is also used alternatively with chief priests and scribes and Pharisees, indicating an identification between the *Ioudaioi* and these leaders or specific groups (see 7:32 and 35; 9:13, 16; and 18:22). So the meaning of *Ioudaioi* in the Gospel is not uniform. It is not an all-inclusive term as "Jews" is in our common usage.

In John's Gospel we enter a world in which one can be a Jew and a believer in Jesus Messiah (we would say Christian but they did not). We enter a world in which there is diversity among Jews, and following the destruction of the Temple in 70 C.E., competition and differences in defining the identity and future of the people Israel. When we hear or read about "the Jews" in Newer Testament literature, we must always ask, "Which Jews?" The writers do not always tell us which ones they meant, because they knew which ones they meant. But we do not know, and we tend to read our own realities back into the first century. The antagonism toward "the Jews" in the Gospel of John does not necessarily mean that the Johannine community was anti-Jewish or that Christians had separated from Judaism.

The Synagogue

The so-called expulsion from the synagogue in the Fourth Gospel contributes to the common perception that the Johannine community no longer identified with the synagogue and was hostile toward Jews. Exclusion of believers from the synagogue is mentioned three times in John. The first appears in the story of the healing of the blind man in which the man's parents refuse to confess that Jesus has healed their son because "they were afraid of the Jews; for the Jews had already agreed that anyone who confessed Jesus to be the Messiah would be put out of the synagogue" (9:22). According to 12:42, many Jews believed in Jesus, but "because of the Pharisees they did not confess it, for fear that they would be put out of the synagogue." And in the farewell discourses (13:1—17:26), Jesus tells his disciples, "They will put you out of the synagogues" (16:2). These references to the expulsion from the synagogue relate to the final composition of the Gospel in the last decade of the first century, of course, and not to the time of Jesus.[4]

In the late 1970s, J. Louis Martyn proposed what became a widely held view among scholars regarding the expulsion from the synagogue. He connected the expulsion mentioned in John with the *birkat haminim*, the so-called "benediction against heretics" included in the Eighteen Benedictions supposedly developed at the rabbinic academy at Jamnia around 90 C.E. Martyn argued that the *birkat haminim* was widely used in synagogue liturgy for the purpose of exposing "Christians" and excluding them from the synagogue. According to Martyn, the Johannine community members belonged to the synagogue; their ejection represented a decisive split after which they, and other believers, were not welcome in the synagogue and no longer identified themselves as Jews.[5] Martyn places the expulsion alluded to in John in the wider context of a supposed schism between Judaism and Christianity. According to this explanation, John is indeed anti-Jewish. It also places the responsibility for the anti-Judaism on the synagogue, the Jews themselves. They initiated the conflict, rejecting both the "Christians" and their claims about Jesus, so the hostility toward the Jews was justified.

The argument that the *birkat haminim* explains the expulsion from the synagogue and the hostility toward the Jews has not held up to the scrutiny of scholarship in the last twenty years. There is no evidence that the Eighteen Benedictions were formulated at the rabbinic council at Jamnia (Javneh), nor that the benediction against "heretics" was directed at followers of Jesus Christ, nor that they were widely used in synagogues throughout Judea or Galilee or the Diaspora. There is no mention of the Benedictions in John, linking them with the experience of the Johannine community, nor is there evidence for widespread "anti-Christian" activity that would provide a likely context for the eviction from the synagogue.[6]

While the "benediction against the heretics" has not held up to careful investigation, it nevertheless remains a popular explanation and justification for the hostility toward Jews and Judaism in John.[7] But even apart from the *birkat haminim,* the simple fact that John mentions an expulsion from the synagogue "for fear of the Jews" implies to modern ears that the Jews were responsible for the eviction of the "christians" because of their beliefs about Jesus, and that this provides the historical reason for the decisive parting of the ways between Jews and Christians. The blame for the schism falls upon the Jews.

The references in John to an eviction of those who publicly confessed Jesus as Messiah refer to an experience of the Johannine community alone. We cannot infer from their situation a universal and decisive schism between Jews and Christians. But even within the Gospel of John, the conflict with the synagogue does not necessarily indicate anti-Judaism. Given the diversity of early Judaism and the ambiguity concerning the definition of *Ioudaioi,* a more nuanced interpretation is required for the author's assertion that some who believed kept quiet because they were afraid "the Jews" would put them out of the synagogue. Both internal and external evidence points to an intra-Jewish controversy.

According to John, there is indeed a conflict between the synagogue leaders and the Johannine community. From the perspective of the Gospel writer, the conflict appears to center on the commu-nity's claims about Jesus. The blind man's parents refuse to come to the defense of their son because it would involve acknowledging messianic claims about Jesus, which would result in their eviction from the synagogue (9:22); and many who believed in Jesus, even among the religious authorities, did not confess it because the consequence would be exclusion from the synagogue. But it is unlikely that simply expressing a belief in the identity of Jesus as Messiah would necessarily result in being tossed out of the synagogue community. Jews often disagreed over matters of belief and practice that did not lead to schisms. We must inquire further why claims about Jesus would have resulted in the eviction of followers of Jesus from the synagogue, resulted in the *experience* of exclusion on the part of the Johannine community, which are not necessarily the same thing.

David Reed argues that the historical circumstances behind the expulsion of the messianists were likely more political than religious. He notes the anti-imperial rhetoric in the Fourth Gospel.[8] The titles ascribed to Jesus assert Jesus' sovereignty. He is called "Lord," and "Savior of the World," and in the trial narrative (chapters 18–19) accepts the title "King." These titles are also ascribed to the Caesars of the Roman Empire. Such language would have made the Johannine community vulnerable to Roman suspicions, and their presence in the synagogue would have made the synagogue vulnerable to the threat of Roman retaliation as well. John's narrative of the trial before Pilate lends support to the argument that fear of antagonizing Rome was a factor in the synagogue leaders' decision to exclude members of the Johannine community. According to John, the *Ioudaioi* charge Pilate with disloyalty to the emperor if he releases Barabbas: "If you release this man, you are no friend of the emperor" (19:12a). And they charge Jesus (implicating his followers of the late first century) with opposition to Rome: "Everyone who claims to be a king sets himself against the emperor" (19:12b). In John's narrative, the chief priests' rejection of Jesus and pronouncement of loyalty to Rome amounts to blasphemy: "We have no king but the emperor" (19:15). The God of Israel is king, and from the perspective of the author, Jesus is God's Messiah, or anointed king. John's portrayal of the *Ioudaioi* and their leaders focuses on their allegiance to Rome as a reason for their rejection of Jesus.

According to Reed's reconstruction, the proclamation of Jesus had unmistakable political overtones. He argues that "there is something in John's overall message, whether from him or his community or a combination of the two, which struck right at the heart of Rome, because the message was anti-imperial."[9] The presence of believers in the synagogue posed a threat because they used anti-imperial language to make claims about the sovereignty of Jesus. So the synagogue leaders understandably chose to distance themselves from those whose presence in their midst made the synagogue vulnerable. Reed suggests that we might empathize with the synagogue leaders rather than cast them in a negative light. Further, he proposes that their actions may have had a positive effect by "quelling the anti-imperialistic rhetoric of the Christians [*sic*], a rhetoric that had the possibility of rousing Rome's ire and leading to the dark path of destruction as it had already done in the recent past or would do once again in the very near future."[10]

The Gospel narrative does not indicate that there was a "witch hunt" to expose and expel believers. John implies that those who believed in Jesus could remain in the synagogue if they did not openly confess Jesus. The blind man's parents and many *Ioudaioi*, including leaders, chose silence rather than exclusion from the synagogue community. Joseph of Arimathea was a believer but a secret one "for fear of the Jews"; presumably fearing the synagogue leaders and exclusion (19:38). Nicodemus, a Pharisee, recognized Jesus' identity at night, but did not confess it openly (3:1; 7:45-50; 19:39). Since believers could remain in the synagogue community if they kept silent, we must wonder what the believers did in the synagogue to provoke expulsion. Were they very vocal? Were they insistent that all must confess Jesus as Messiah as they did? Were they divisive? These questions invite us at least to consider the situation from the point of view of the synagogue leaders and for a moment to empathize with them. Can we imagine that there might have been some justification for insisting that a vocal minority either keep quiet or leave?

When we reconstruct the historical circumstances surrounding the expulsion from the synagogue, we might consider also the possibility that the Gospel narrative describes the community's experience of exclusion and marginalization from the synagogue community more than a decisive action by the synagogue. The author's hostility toward the *Ioudaioi*, the synagogue leaders in particular, may reflect the pain of dislocation, of loss of community through one's own choices, more than a decision systematically to evict believers from the synagogue. If we could ask one of the synagogue leaders why he adopted the policy of evicting believers from the synagogue, he might be surprised. "Put them out?" he might say. "Oh, we didn't do that. There are definitely some differences among us, and we did ask some of them to keep quiet and respect the views of others or we would ask them to leave." From the perspective of the author, this might have been tantamount to expulsion. In fact, the Gospel narrative casts an unfavorable light on those "closet believers" who keep silent in order to remain in the synagogue community. The Gospel writer advocates confessing Jesus as Messiah openly regardless of the consequences. The Gospel account indicates that not all in the community of believers agreed. This imaginative reconstruction simply suggests the possibility that the Gospel narrative reflects the experience and convictions of the Johannine community and may exaggerate the events that contributed to the situation. We remember, too, that we do not have the perspective of the local synagogue, or even from those believers who remained in the synagogue.

Our perception of the synagogue in the late first century influences how we interpret the expulsion from the synagogue mentioned in the Fourth Gospel. When we imagine the synagogue as an established institution perpetuating the traditions of Israel, vesting its leaders with power and authority to define Judaism, it is very easy to read John as anti-Jewish and to justify its anti-Judaism. The believers' expulsion from the synagogue corroborates the assumption that the well-established synagogue easily eliminated any challenge to Jewish orthodoxy. But in the decades following the destruction of the Temple, rabbinic Judaism had not yet established itself as the dominant voice within Judaism. The synagogue communities were engaged in the process of identity formation. They did not have a definition of Judaism clearly worked out, so the idea that they could easily enforce a particular position and evict those who did not conform is anachronistic. Also, Jewish communities were vulnerable to Roman persecution in the period following the Jewish War against Rome. One of the mistakes modern interpreters of the Newer Testament frequently make is that we do not see the presence of Rome. We attribute power and authority to Jews in situations in which they are relatively powerless in relation to the imperial power of Rome.

The Gospel of John witnesses to some serious conflict between the Johannine community and synagogue leaders that, according to the narrative, resulted in the expulsion of believers from the synagogue. We do not know the historical realities of that conflict. Traditional historical reconstructions conclude that the Gospel's author was anti-Jewish, and that the anti-Judaism was justified. But a careful reading of the different meanings of *Ioudaioi* in the Gospel and the imprecise boundaries between *Ioudaioi* and the Johannine community of believers lead us to understand the expulsion from the synagogue in light of a complex intra-Jewish controversy.

Sectarianism

The question of sectarianism in the Gospel of John is not a new one. The answer to whether John represents sectarianism or not depends on how one defines a sect, and scholars have differed on the answer.[11] David Rensberger adopts a sociological definition. Sociologist Thomas Johnson cites twelve characteristics of a sectarian community, and several of them relate to the Fourth Gospel.[12] For example, a sect regards the world as evil and withdraws from the world. We see this withdrawal from the world in several places in John. According to 15:18-19, Jesus tells his disciples, "If the world hates you, be aware that it hated me before it hated you. If you belonged to the world, the world would love you as its own. Because you do not belong to the world, but I have chosen you out of the world—therefore the world hates you." Alienation from the world is a theme in chapter 17: "I have given them your word, and the world has hated them because they do not belong to the world, just as I do not belong to the world. I am not asking you to take them out of the world, but I ask you to protect them from the evil one" (vv. 14-15). The characteristic sectarian claim to a unique or special truth is evident in John. According to 14:6, Jesus is the only way one comes to know God. And 3:16-19 professes that those who believe in God's only Son have eternal life and those who do not believe are condemned.

Voluntary membership in a sect is based on special religious experience or knowledge. We see evidence of this in the Nicodemus story. Nicodemus comes to see Jesus by night, recognizes him as a teacher from God, but he does not grasp the special experience of being born anew and does not receive the community's testimony (3:1-21). And after Jesus drives the sellers and money changers out of the Temple, when the *Ioudaioi* ask him for a sign, he replies, "Destroy this temple, and in three days I will raise it up" (2:19). The *Ioudaioi* do not understand that Jesus was speaking of "the temple of his body" (2:21) but the disciples remembered, after Jesus' resurrection, that he had said this and they believed (2:22).

As a sect withdraws from the world, it typically creates an intimate fellowship among members. We see this in John, in the metaphor of the good shepherd who knows his sheep, knows them by name, the sheep follow him because they know his voice, and they do not follow a stranger's voice (10:1-18). The intimate fellowship is evident also in the metaphor of the true vine, particularly in the repetition of the image "abide in me and I in you" (15:1-11). Jesus' command to the community to love one another, even to the point of giving one's life, and calling them friends also indicate the Johannine community's self-understanding as a tightly knit group separate from others. A dualistic view of reality is a characteristic sectarian perspective and one that is evident in John. We see the contrast between light and darkness (1:1-9; 3:19-21; 8:12); good and evil (3:19-21); blindness and sight (9:1-41); belief and unbelief (3:16-19); truth and falsehood. The dualism between "us" and "them," manifested especially in the polemic against "the Jews," is typical of a sectarian view of the world.

The Johannine community fits a sociological definition of a sect. The narrative of John witnesses to a community alienated from the world and separated from the synagogue and from some other believers as well. The loss of the synagogue was apparently acute, and the community turned inward and defined itself over and against the local synagogue. The Johannine community was a sect within Judaism and in relationship to the dominant culture of Judaism in its location. This accounts for the sharp polemic against "the Jews." The polemic, in this sectarian context, identifies the community and legitimates its claims against all others.

Summary

Is the Gospel of John anti-Jewish? I do not think so. I do not think that the Gospel narrative points to an author or a community that perceived itself as irrevocably separated from Judaism. The ambiguity with respect to the meaning of *Ioudaioi* in the first-century world and the diverse meanings assigned to *Ioudaioi* within the narrative suggest that *Ioudaioi* was not an all-encompassing term that distinguishes Jews from Christians, the way that it sounds to our ears. And while the Gospel writer blames "the Jews" for throwing the believers out of the synagogue, the circumstances for their ejection is not at all clear. The narrative does indicate, however, that some believers chose to stay in the synagogue, so we cannot conclude that there was a concerted effort to expose them, and we must consider the possibility that some Jews did not think it was necessary to choose between the synagogue community and belief in the messiahship of Jesus. The writer clearly does not include all Jews in his polemic against the synagogue leaders. Finally, the narrative indicates a sect within Judaism defining itself in relationship to the dominant culture of Judaism, following the destruction of the Temple, within the context of formative Judaism, before the separation between Judaism and Christianity.

Hearing with Modern Ears

The author of the Fourth Gospel may not have been anti-Jewish, but the Gospel sounds anti-Jewish to our ears. Making the case that the Johannine community was not separate from first-century Judaism does not solve the problem of John and anti-Judaism. In any public reading of John we inevitably encounter Judaism as we understand it. When we hear, for example, that "the disciples were hiding for fear of the Jews," we identify Jews as a threat to the followers of Christ. When Jesus calls Jewish antagonists a "child of the devil," our ears hear the plain meaning, that all, or most, Jews who did not follow Jesus were enemies of the movement that became Christianity. According to John's Passion narrative, the Jews demand Jesus' crucifixion in spite of Pilate's failure to find in Jesus any offense, thus reinforcing the guilt of the Jews for the crucifixion. Because of the intensified polemic against the Jews, simply reading and hearing this Gospel reinforces traditional Christian anti-Judaism. Whereas the Synoptic Gospels indicate conflicts with particular groups within Judaism, John implies to modern hearers the guilt of all Jews. So when a passage from the Fourth Gospel is assigned or selected, the first task for the preacher or worship leader is deciding what to read.

It is ironic that modern Bible translations, which seek to make ancient texts understandable to modern audiences, have given little attention to the way a misunderstanding of Judaism is transmitted to readers. Recent translations have attended to modern sensibilities about sexism by using inclusive language rather than gender-specific words ("brothers and sisters" rather than "brothers"; "people" or "humankind" rather than "men"); several have moved from a "word-for-word" to a "meaning-for-meaning" translation in order to communicate effectively the meaning of the ancient writings for contemporary audiences. Yet, as David Burke observes, "the *hoi Ioudaioi* passages that undergird and encourage anti-Jewish hatred

are a prime example of the chasm that is created by the very translations that seek to unite the centuries."[13]

Some translations do offer a more nuanced translation of *hoi
Ioudaioi*, attentive to the modern meaning of "the Jews" as an all-
inclusive term and label for those who opposed Jesus and the early
"christians." The Contemporary English Version tends to remove
the implication that all Jews were antagonistic toward the followers of Jesus and, later, the churches. For example, in John 18:20, the
NRSV translates *pantes hoi Ioudaioi* as "all the Jews," a straightfor-
ward word-for-word translation, whereas the CEV translates "all of
our people." The NRSV translates John 11:54, "Jesus therefore no
longer walked about openly among the Jews," whereas the CEV reads
"stopped going around in public." The CEV translates 18:31, "the
crowd replied" rather than "the Jews replied," and throughout the
Passion narrative, the CEV renders *hoi Ioudaioi* as "the crowd" or
"the people."[14] The CEV editors contend that they are faithful to the
intention of the authors in the way they translate *Ioudaioi*. Joseph
Blenkinsopp argues, however, that the negative attitudes in Christian texts should not be sanitized, and he alleges that the CEV translators attempt to remedy the problem of anti-Judaism by making
the authors say what they did not intend.[15] The difference of opinion centers on the understanding of the first-century context and
whether or not the writers represent a Christianity separated from
Judaism or communities still within Judaism. For my part, I think
the CEV is a good "meaning-for-meaning" translation with respect
to conveying first-century realities.

Gerard Sloyan advocates leaving *Ioudaioi* untranslated when we
read the Fourth Gospel in public settings and preach on Johannine
texts. His rationale is that we simply do not know which *Ioudaioi*
the writer meant, and because, while the Gospel writer did not
mean all Jews, Christians tend to identify all Jewish people with
the "some Jews" in John.[16] Sloyan acknowledges that this approach
is reasonable only for the preacher who is regularly with the same
congregation week after week, but in this situation the usage of the
untranslated Greek heightens awareness of the tendency to make
assumptions about Jews and Judaism that are inaccurate. Sloyan's
motive for leaving *Ioudaioi* untranslated is a concern for modern
anti-Judaism:

> Modern preachers and teachers need to be on guard against making an easy target of *any* people or class by careless rhetoric. This they do by using the translation "the Jews" unexamined. The woeful failure of Christian preachers over twenty centuries to make careful distinctions whenever they speak of the Jews in a first-century context has made this a question apart.[17]

Sloyan's final point is the critical one. Whether one chooses to leave *Ioudaioi* untranslated or not, the failure to make distinctions among Jews, even when an English translation does not, simply reinforces misunderstanding at best, and anti-Judaism at worst.

I recommend that preachers compare a few authorized translations in preparation for reading and preaching from John. This will provide insights into the interpretations of others (translations *are* interpretations!) and possibilities for understanding the particular meaning of *Ioudaioi* in a particular passage. One might choose a translation that is sensitive to the issues, or one might emend a translation by borrowing a phrase from another. I have done this when reading John 20:19. Where the NRSV translates "for fear of the Jews," I read "for fear of the Judeans" in accordance with several authorized translations. Regardless of what one chooses to read, the sermon will most likely bear the burden of addressing in some way the anti-Judaism we hear.

Preaching on the Fourth Gospel

The first task for the preacher is simply to be alert to the complexities of John and the ways we easily misconstrue its meaning when we hear the polemic against "the Jews." The second is to resist the temptation of using Jews or Jewish groups as a foil: the blind Pharisees, the Jewish authorities, the synagogue leaders, the Jews who question Jesus. A sermon might include at least a few sentences reminding us that all the people in the narrative were first-century Jews, that the Jews themselves were a minority and all were vulnerable to the imperial power of Rome, that the writer is not critical of all Jews and that he is disapproving of some believers, and, when appropriate, that the conflict within the synagogue was likely a complex one and almost certainly does not mean that all synagogues expelled all "christians." The question for the preacher is: How do we tell the truth John tells in the first century in the twenty-first century?

A method I often use in preaching on controversies or polemical texts is to develop a sympathetic view to each of the parties in the controversy or to the objects of the polemic. I imagine what the situation described in the text might look like from the vantage point of different participants in a controversy. This invites us to consider perspectives other than the narrator's view. There are two distinct advantages to this approach. The first is that we open ourselves and our listeners to what might be at stake for the Gospel writer and early believing communities that might not be immediately obvious to us. And second, listeners are encouraged to hear the situation in terms of the complexities of our own lives in religious communities in which we differ in our discernment concerning what God is about in our lives, in our churches, in our world.

The following is a sermon I preached on the story of Jesus' healing of the blind man in the ninth chapter of John. Because the narrative is the entire chapter, I did not read the Gospel prior to the sermon. The sermon incorporated a reading of the Gospel with a running commentary.

As [Jesus] walked along, he saw a man blind from birth. His disciples asked him, "Rabbi, who sinned, this man or his parents, that he was born blind?" Jesus answered, "Neither this man nor his parents sinned; he was born blind so that God's works might be revealed in him."

The perennial question: Why? What caused it? What is the reason for this affliction, this tragedy? The disciples reflect the thought of their time, that there is a connection between sin and affliction, cause and effect. While we might not think in terms of sin, the cause-and-effect logic is familiar. Why did cancer strike this one? Poor diet? Not enough exercise? Exposure to suspect chemicals? If we can explain it, we can control it and thus protect ourselves. Jesus' answer may not be satisfactory for us either, if we're honest. You mean that God planned this man's blindness so that Jesus could demonstrate his power? Perhaps Jesus' answer might be taken another way: the man's blindness just is. It happened. But God's presence may be revealed even through suffering, affliction, unfortunate circumstances, such as this blind man's birth defect. And so Jesus, God's human agent, goes to work saying, "As long as I am in the world, I am the light of the world."

When he had said this, he spat on the ground and made mud with saliva and spread the mud on the man's eyes, saying to him, "Go, wash in the pool of Siloam" (which means Sent). Then he went and washed and came back able to see. The neighbors and those who had seen him before as a beggar began to ask, "Is this not the man who used to sit and beg?" Some were saying, "It is he." Others were saying, "No, but it is someone like him." He kept saying, "I am the man." But they kept asking him, "Then how were your eyes opened?"

We're not very good at thinking outside the box, are we? We're more willing to believe mistaken identity than the mystery of God at work here. It looks just like him, but it can't be him because he's blind. The man who was blind is exceedingly patient in the story. He answered, "The man called Jesus made mud, spread it on my eyes, and said to me, 'Go to Siloam and wash.' Then I went and washed and received my sight." They said to him, "Where is he?" He said, "I do not know."

Change of scene. Begin scene two. Unwilling to accept the man's simple explanation. . . . They brought to the Pharisees the man who had formerly been blind. Now it was a Sabbath day when Jesus made the mud and opened his eyes. That's important, because as we will see, if we are willing to see, that the Pharisees are quite open to seeing God at work.

Then the Pharisees also began to ask him how he had received his sight. Polite and interested. He said to them, "He put mud on my eyes. Then I washed, and now I see." Still patient. Some of the Pharisees said, "This man [meaning Jesus] is not from God, for he does not observe the Sabbath." But others said, "How can a man who is a sinner perform such signs?" And they were divided. The Pharisees were accustomed to perceiving God's presence in the world. God was revealed through the sacred time of the Sabbath, so one who ignored the Sabbath dismissed divinely ordained sacred time. But they also recognized that healing, certainly the gift of sight, came from God, also a divinely ordained act. What had happened to the blind man must be a sign of God's healing power. They disagreed. (I might add here that there was no law against healing on the Sabbath when there was good reason, and the Pharisees recognized lots of good reasons, but the man had been blind from birth, so presumably the healing might have waited a few more hours until the Sabbath ended at sunset.) So they said again to the blind man, "What do you say about him? It was your eyes he opened." He said, "He is a prophet."

Scene change. Back to the people. They had a hard time believing that the man had been blind his whole life and had suddenly received his sight. So they called the parents of the man who had been blind and now could see and asked them, "Is this your son, who you say was born blind? How then does he now see?" His parents answered, "We know that this is our son, and that he was born blind; but we do not know how it is that now he sees, nor do we know who opened his eyes. Ask him; he is of age. He will speak for himself."

The parents clear up the matter of the man's identity. He is their son who was born blind. But they fall short of clearing up the real problem. How did it happen? Don't they know that it was Jesus who opened the eyes of their son? Don't they believe their son, who told them the story he has repeated for anyone who has asked? Don't they see? They do see, but they are unwilling to risk the consequences of telling what they believe to be true. For, according to the story, his parents said this because they were afraid, for their community had already agreed that anyone who confessed Jesus to be the Messiah would be asked to leave.

Now I know if you know this story very well or if you happen to be reading along, the Bible says, "They were afraid of the Jews; for the Jews had already agreed that anyone who confessed Jesus to be the Messiah would be put out of the synagogue." But when we read it that way we miss the point, because to our ears it sounds as though Jews rejected Christians and kicked them out of the synagogue because Jews rejected Jesus as Messiah. We miss the fact that <u>this was a family crisis.</u> All the people in the story are Jews. Obviously the parents think they belonged in the synagogue, and they want to be there, so much so that they disassociated themselves from their son. We sense that they do believe that Jesus is indeed God's Messiah, but the risk of saying so would mean alienation from friends and family, the loss of their community. The loss is too great. Therefore, the parents of the blind man said, "Ask him; he is of age. He will speak for himself."

The parents of the blind man who now sees do not come off well in the story. The reader is not supposed to sympathize with them, but I do. And, of course, the Jews of the synagogue are the antagonists and the narrator certainly does not invite the reader to think kindly of them, but I empathize with them, too. Imagine what it would be like for us if some of us confronted our community in worship regularly with a behavior or article of faith that was contrary to how many of us understand the truth about God. Wouldn't we eventually lose patience *and simply say, "Look, if you are not in agreement with our customs and beliefs here, why don't you find another place to worship where you will be more comfortable?" Haven't we said that at times, if not directly, at least implied it? Or haven't we at times kept our doubts or our convictions to ourselves rather than risk the disapproval of others in the community? Perhaps we might see ourselves in both the parents and the synagogue leaders in the story.*

Having received no satisfactory response from the parents, a second time they called the man who had been blind, and they said to him, "Give glory to God! [Or, in other words, "Tell the truth!"] We know that this man [meaning Jesus] is a sinner." They've concluded that this is the only logical answer, though they seem open to the blind man's answer. He answered, maybe not quite so patiently as before, "I do not know whether he is a sinner. One thing I do know, that though I was blind, now I see." They said to him, "What did he do to you? How did he open your eyes?" He answered them, "I have told you already, and you would not listen. Why do you want to hear it again? Do you also want to become his disciples?"

Oh, now he's gone too far. Then they reviled him, saying, "You are his disciple, but we are disciples of Moses. We know that God has spoken to Moses, but as for this man, we do not know where he comes from." The man answered, "Here is an astonishing thing! You do not know where he comes from, and yet he opened my eyes. We all know that God does not listen to sinners, don't we, but God does listen to one who worships him and obeys his will. Never since the world began has it been heard that anyone opened the eyes of a person born blind. If this man were not from God, he could do nothing."

This is the man's concluding confession, which actually echoes the insights of those Pharisees who ask the question, "Yes, but how can a man who is a sinner perform such signs?" It is a rhetorical question that implies the inevitable conclusion that Jesus is not a sinner at all, but restoring the blind man's sight is a sign revealing God's presence in their midst. But this is not the insight that prevails on this day. How difficult it is to allow for new insights that do not conform to what we already know. The people said to him, "You were born entirely in sin, and are you trying to teach us?" And they drove him out.

Enter Jesus, who has been absent from the scene since he spit on the ground, made mud, rubbed in the blind man's eyes, and gave him sight. Jesus heard that they had driven him out, and when he found him he said, "Do you believe in the Son of Man?" He answered, "And who is he, sir? Tell me, so that I may believe in him." (Evidently he does not see everything so clearly, even yet.) Jesus said to him, "You have seen him, and the one speaking with you is he." He said, "Lord [or maybe it is "sir;" the Greek word is the same], I believe." And he worshiped him. Jesus then said, "I came into this world for judgment (or we might say "to create a crisis that provokes discernment") so that those who do not see may see, and those who do see may become blind." Some of the Pharisees near him heard this and said to him, "Surely we are not blind, are we?"

Are we? Those who are blind see the best. Those who know don't see. Those who know and might see may be unwilling or unable to risk what they know in order to see more clearly. Blessed are those who see, know what they see, and believe.[18]

The strategy of entering into a story imaginatively through a person whom the writer casts in an unfavorable light works in the narrative featuring Nicodemus's visit to Jesus at night (John 3:1-15). Nicodemus is described as a Pharisee and leader of the Jews, and though he recognizes Jesus as a "teacher come from God" he does not fully understand Jesus' identity nor fully accept the witness of the believers. In a sermon on this text, I described Nicodemus as a seeker and invited the congregation to relate to him as one seeking to know more, understand more deeply, pointing out that Nicodemus did seek out Jesus and that his journey led him to be present to care for Jesus' body after the crucifixion (19:39).

In a different interpretation of this narrative, I took the narrator's point of view in criticizing Nicodemus as a "closet believer." Nicodemus functions in the Gospel as a representative of the secret believers in the Johannine community who refuse to be public in confessing their belief in Jesus Christ (like the blind man's parents).[19] In this sermon I challenged the listeners to consider ways that, like Nicodemus, we choose not to speak about our faith, and ways that we might be more open and vocal in articulating our Christian beliefs rather than allowing others to define the public perception of Christian values. In both sermons, I encouraged the listeners to identify with Nicodemus, thus resisting the temptation to distance ourselves from the Pharisee and leader of the Jews as a nonbeliever and opponent of "christians."

The beginning of the Fourth Gospel sounds to Christian ears like a proclamation of the divine nature of Jesus and the high Christology we associate with John. It is easy, therefore, to miss the continuity between the prologue of John (1:1-18) and Israel's Scriptures. Here is an opportunity for the preacher to ground the gospel's proclamation in Israel's Scriptures and take a more theocentric approach to John than is typical. What follows is the beginning of a sermon in which I interpret the prologue as a kind of midrash on Genesis 1:

> It was meant to be. . . . In the beginning. . . . we are meant to hear the echoes of Genesis. The poetry of the prologue intends to echo the poetry of Genesis. In the beginning there was darkness, and God said let there be light. In the beginning was the Word . . . the light of all people. The light shines in the darkness and the darkness did not overcome it. It was meant to be that the Word would take on flesh and dwell among us. Inevitable, given God's love for the world, God's investment in human affairs, God's choosing a particular people through which to be known, initiating a covenant with Abraham, righteous law given through Moses, interpreted through the prophets. Given God's history, God's ever-drawing closer, God's self-giving love . . . it was meant to be that in the fullness of time the Word would take on flesh and live among us.
>
> This is what John says in poetic speech. In the beginning, God so loved the world he created that his self-giving was unbounded. When God said, "Let there be light," God meant for there to be light. God was determined that there would be light in this world, even if God's very self must be the light, the light of all people which darkness cannot hide. And so the Word which was in the beginning creating became flesh and lived among us, and we have seen the fullness of God's glory, received the fullness of grace, in a way so unexpected and yet now that we think about it we might have anticipated, knowing God's story from the beginning, and so we say: it was meant to be. And we say God's coming into the world in Jesus occurs in the fullness of time, meaning: what more could we possibly expect from God?[20]

The sermon emphasized the revelation of God in Christ within the whole of God's story and explored issues of discerning God's presence among us, a light in the darkness, an appropriate theme for the first Sunday after Christmas when lectionaries annually assign John 1:18.

Taking Sectarianism Seriously

The sectarianism in John presents challenges for the preacher. The polarity between insiders and outsiders, isolationism, and exclusive claims to truth are characteristic of sects and part of the Johannine world, yet it is unlikely that we would recommend Christians emulate these traits. When these themes are present in the text, the preacher might briefly put them in context so that listeners have a way of understanding without appropriating them literally or rejecting them as irrelevant. But not all aspects of sectarianism are negative. David Rensberger advocates that we take seriously the sectarianism of John: "For I want us to bear in mind that the church is never more true to itself than when it remembers its origin as a sect, as a minority opinion, countercultural and antiestablishment." He does not intend that we adopt first-century sectarianism nor does he dismiss its negative tendencies, but he does suggest that the church is much too comfortable with the status quo and has lost its ability "to present a fundamental challenge to the world's oppressive orders."[21] He advocates adopting the role of minority opinion and thus "take a stand over against the world and to criticize that which the world holds most dear."[22] I find Rensberger's observations very useful for preaching. He reminds us that John's view was a minority opinion within Judaism in the first century and offers a positive way for Christians to consider that role in our own times.

Telling John's Truth

How do we tell the truth John tells in our own time? First, we must be shocked by what we read and hear in this Gospel. I wonder if the first challenge we encounter is that the polemic against the Jews sounds "right" to most of us in its familiarity. Barbara Brown Taylor's response, cited above, is a good place to begin: "There are whole chapters of John's Gospel that I would like to snip right out of the book so that no child ever has to read what John said Jesus said about Jews."[23] Second, in order to tell the truth John tells, we need to hear the narrative within its first-century context. I am convinced that the author perceived himself and community within Judaism, a minority increasingly alienated from the prevailing orientation of Judaism but not separated from Judaism. This construction of context opens abundant possibilities for homiletical interpretation of the Fourth Gospel. But even if one concludes that the Johannine community identified itself as "Christian," separated from Judaism and thus anti-Jewish, this does not grant license to adopt this view in our own communities. Our history and its complicity in anti-Judaism demand that we name it and distance ourselves from it.

Finally, the preacher must take time to tell the truth John tells. An obstacle for those of us who follow lectionaries is that they do not assign the Fourth Gospel for extended periods during the church year. Perhaps we might occasionally adopt the rubric "The lectionary was made for the church, not the church for the lectionary" and depart from the designated Gospel reading for a series of sermons on John. For those with more flexibility in worship planning, devoting a series to the Gospel of John is theoretically easier. Nevertheless, it requires a commitment to address the challenges of interpreting this Gospel. But since our Bibles include a Fourth Gospel, we have a responsibility to rise to the challenge.

5

The Passion Narrative

MEL GIBSON'S MOVIE *The Passion of the Christ* has drawn extraordinary attention to the central narrative of the Christian Gospels. Leading up to and following the release of the movie on Ash Wednesday 2004, weekly news magazines featured articles about it, biblical scholars debated its merits, churches reserved theaters to see it, and others refused to see it. Regardless of one's opinion of the movie, it created a teaching moment. In classrooms, parish adult-education forums, and organized panel discussions, Christians discussed questions regarding the meaning of Jesus' death and about how and why he died. We considered the Gospel stories of Jesus' Passion both from the perspective of Christian faith and historical accuracy. And Christians involved in conversations with Jewish friends and colleagues listened to how they hear the Passion story in light of their own history.

After seeing *The Passion of the Christ* and observing its popularity, Rabbi Barry Cytron expressed his fears: "I'm afraid that all the progress we've made [toward mutual understanding between Jews and Christians] will be lost."[1] His concerns were echoed by other prominent American Jewish leaders who witnessed the full theaters and acclaim for the movie by many Christian groups. They wondered what effect the movie's stereotypical portrayal of Jews would have on Christian viewers. Some Christians dismissed their concerns as an overreaction. Others paid attention to how Jews experienced the cultural phenomenon of this movie.

In Jewish history, Christian Holy Week is inexorably linked with persecution. In Christian Europe, Jews associated Good Friday with pogroms; they learned to expect acts of vengeance by Christians who had been aroused by the story of Christ's Passion. Civilized

Christians presume that this is ancient history. Jews know that it is not. The charge of deicide is part of the Christian story in the holiest week of the Christian year. Passion plays often heighten the culpability of the Jewish religious leaders along with the crowds. To be sure, most mainstream Christian churches have formal statements denouncing the charge of deicide, and the Vatican has issued guidelines for the production of Passion plays to counter the misconception of Jewish guilt.[2] Christian liturgical and biblical scholars have made available Passion narrative readings for congregational use that take care not to distort first-century realities in contemporary contexts. But Gibson's movie does not follow Vatican guidelines, nor does it take into account first-century contexts. And it appears that the majority of Christians took Gibson at his word, that he simply told the story according to the Gospels, and further, that the Gospel truth and the historical truth are inseparable. Concern on the part of Jewish observers is understandable.

In an essay on Mel Gibson's movie, Rabbi Michael Lerner observed that "if Christians have not confronted anti-Judaism as effectively as they have tackled other 'isms,' then that is because doing so requires them to question the historical truth of their own scriptures."[3] I think he is right. But what is at stake here is not simply the historical truth of the Scriptures. The problem is that anti-Judaism is most critical precisely where the historical truth of the Gospels is most vital *and* reliable. No one seriously doubts that Jesus was executed by crucifixion under procurator Pontius Pilate when Caiaphas was high priest and Tiberius was emperor. For Christians this historical fact matters. Historical truth and Gospel truth coincide at this point in the Passion narrative. The historical truth of the Gospels matters here in a way that is more essential than in other details of the Gospel story. Yet, because the Passion narrative is at the root of a long Christian history of fratricide, Christians must consider carefully and critically how the Gospel accounts of Jesus' last days in Jerusalem weave together historical facts and theological interpretation of historical events in an apparently seamless narrative.

History Remembered and History Interpreted

The Passion narratives of the Gospels seem to be a continuous historical narrative, and yet there are parts of the story that are undoubtedly historically reliable, and other parts of the story that very likely did not happen as the story tells it. Certainly Jesus was crucified under Roman rule when Pilate was procurator of Judea. But it is improbable, for example, that Pilate conversed with Jesus before ordering his death, or that Pilate offered to release Jesus but yielded to the crowds' univocal demand to crucify him and release Barabbas instead. There is no extra-biblical evidence that there existed a custom of releasing a prisoner during the Passover feast; other primary historical sources corroborate Pilate's cruelty and extreme disdain for the people of Judea, leading to his removal as procurator by the emperor. About other aspects of the story there is uncertainty. Was there a trial by the Sanhedrin? What was the jurisdiction of the religious authorities? What was the role of the crowds? What was the reason for Jesus' death? What details of the story constitute history remembered and what is history interpreted from the perspective of later faith claims about Jesus Messiah? Biblical scholars differ regarding what represents historical truth in the Gospel narratives and what likely is attributable to the interests of a later generation who shaped the Gospel accounts as we have them today. In the last decade, the work of the prominent scholars John Dominic Crossan and Raymond Brown serve to illustrate the complexity of the story of Jesus' suffering and death and why it matters that Christians take seriously questions concerning the historical truth in the Passion narratives.

Raymond Brown's book, *The Death of the Messiah: From Gethsemane to the Grave—A Commentary on the Passion Narratives in the Four Gospels*, was featured in the major weekly news magazines just before Easter 1994.[4] It represents an exhaustive examination of the Gospel accounts of Jesus' death, including questions of historical reliability. Crossan wrote *Who Killed Jesus? Exposing the Roots of Anti-Semitism in the Gospel Story of the Death of Jesus* as a critical response to Brown. According to Crossan, he and Brown agree that the Gospel accounts of Jesus' Passion include both "history remembered" and "prophecy historicized."[5] They differ considerably, though, regarding how much is "history remembered" and how much is "prophecy historicized." Crossan believes that the structure of the Gospel narratives is informed by an understanding of Jesus' death as the fulfillment of Israel's Scriptures and that most of the Gospel story is "prophecy historicized," that is, the fulfillment of prophecy in the form of historical narrative. Brown, on the other hand, regards much more of the Gospel accounts as "history remembered." Crossan's sharpest criticism of Brown, however, is for his failure to make historical judgments about features of the story that are historically plausible, or credible, thus implying that if something could have happened or might have happened, then likely it did happen.

According to Crossan, this is not merely an academic debate.

> There may well be some stories in the New Testament that one can leave as "maybe historical" and avoid asserting one's best historical judgment or reconstruction about them. But the passion-resurrection stories are different because they have been the seedbed for Christian anti-Judaism. And without that Christian anti-Judaism, lethal and genocidal European anti-Semitism would have been either impossible or at least not widely successful. What was at stake in those passion stories, in the long haul of history, was the Jewish Holocaust.[6]

Brown was certainly aware of the problem of anti-Judaism in relation to the Passion narrative. He addresses this issue explicitly in *The Death of the Messiah*.[7] But at the same time, his scholarship on the Gospels' Passion narratives points to an implicit investment in protecting the historical veracity of the Gospel accounts of Jesus' Passion. Crossan's critique is less in the details of reconstruction than in Brown's reluctance to make historical judgments where Crossan believes there is a moral imperative to do so.

The Brown-Crossan debate is instructive here for preachers and other congregational leaders for several reasons. First, it calls attention to the fact that the Gospel accounts of Jesus' Passion include both remembered historical events and interpretation of those events by later generations who found divine meaning in them. Most seminary-educated church leaders know this but ordinarily do not consider its relevance in preaching. Second, Crossan asserts that what is at stake is essentially the perpetuation of Christian anti-Judaism where it matters the most, and he challenges one of the most respected Newer Testament scholars in recent generations whose competence and integrity are unquestionable. It is tempting, is it not, to assume that the problem of anti-Judaism lies with others who are not as committed as we are about anti-Judaism. But this conversation is among those who express concern for the problem; what is at stake is our own willingness to examine critically our preaching and liturgy during Holy Week with respect to the portrayal of Jewish involvement in the death of Jesus. Third, the differences between two prominent scholars expose in a tangible way the accuracy of Rabbi Lerner's speculation, that Christians have not been as effective in confronting anti-Judaism as other "isms" because it requires us to confront the historical truth of the Gospels, and, we might add, it requires us to do so where it matters the most.[8] Fourth, Crossan's critique offers incentive to consider historical questions so that we are prepared to seize a teaching moment such as the one Gibson's movie provided. Congregational leaders ought to be prepared to offer informed guidance in assessing the relationship between historical reliability and theological interpretation in the Gospel narratives and in a popular cinematic dramatization. Considering the historical questions will also prepare us to overcome some of the difficulties in Holy Week preaching.

Understanding First-Century Realities

The Brown-Crossan debate may also seem daunting to congregational leaders. If two prominent scholars differ so widely regarding what is historically reliable, we might doubt our own capabilities to make informed historical judgments. Our task here is not a detailed reconstruction, however. Our purpose here is to examine how we unwittingly perpetuate anti-Judaism in our preaching and teaching during Holy Week. When we take into account first-century realities, we will be better equipped to distinguish between what is history remembered and what belongs to later interpretation of earlier events. Two historical contexts are relevant for our understanding of the Passion narrative. The first is Judea at the time of Jesus' death and the second is the post-70 C.E. world of the Gospel writers and their communities. When we consider the presence of Roman imperialism and the diversity of early Judaism before and after 70 C.E., we will gain significant insights with respect to the historical roles of Jews in the Gospel accounts.

When Roman rule began in 63 B.C.E. in what had been an independent Israel, the Romans appointed indigenous leaders to positions of local authority. Although Israel had lost autonomy, their leaders were able to manipulate the system and secure benefits of living under the Roman imperial system. By the beginning of the first century c.e., however, Israel was divided and Judea was placed under the direct administration of a Roman procurator. Rome appointed the high priests and the procurator held custody of the priestly vestments. Although Rome granted freedom of religious observance, "it infringed on those privileges often enough to cause deep-seated uneasiness among the Jews."[9]

Pontius Pilate, procurator from 26 to 36 c.e., antagonized Jewish sensibilities by bringing military standards with Roman images into Jerusalem, thus violating the commandment against graven images. Pilate ignored the Jews' request that the standards be removed, threatening to kill the resisters, until the people demonstrated that they were prepared to die rather than allow the presence of Caesar's images.[10] Pilate's confiscation of funds from the Temple treasury further infuriated the people; he infiltrated the angry crowd of protesters with disguised troops to kill them.[11] Pilate was removed from his office and recalled to Rome after he ordered an attack on unarmed Samaritans on a pilgrimage.[12] Primary sources consistently witness to Pilate's ruthlessness and cruelty toward his subjects.

The Roman imperial system did rely on the talents, labor, and skills of local leadership, but in the first century this did not translate into the benefits one might expect. The purpose served was the support of the system. For example, indigenous tax collectors collected Rome's taxes; the tax collectors supported themselves by exacting a surcharge above Rome's levied taxes, thus arousing their neighbors' resentment. (No doubt some supported themselves very well, but not at the expense of Rome.) Those who could read and write, like scribes and perhaps some among the Pharisees, served administrative functions for the Roman bureaucracy. Being useful to the imperial system made one less vulnerable to the arbitrariness of Roman occupiers.

The role of the Sanhedrin under Roman occupation is a good example of the relationship between Rome and local leadership, between political and religious authority. Based on Josephus's account of an incident involving chief priest Ananus, Ellis Rivkin argues persuasively that the Sanhedrin was an ad hoc group convened only by the emperor to serve Rome's interests.[13] According to Josephus, Ananus seized the opportunity between the death of one procurator, Festus, and the arrival of the next, Albinus, to convene the Sanhedrin to accuse James, the brother of Jesus, of transgressing the Law and delivered him to be stoned.[14] People who were strictly observant of the Law were offended. As Josephus tells it:

> They therefore secretly sent to King Agrippa urging him for Ananus had not even been correct in his first step, to order him to desist from any further such actions. Certain of them even went to meet Albinus, who was on his way from Alexandria, and informed him that Ananus had not the authority to convene the Sanhedrin without his consent. Convinced by these words, Albinus angrily wrote to Ananus threatening to take vengeance upon him. King Agrippa, because of Ananus' action, deposed him from the high priesthood which he had held for three months and replaced him with Jesus the son of Damnaeus.[15]

We learn several things from Josephus's account. First, we see the high priest's dependency on Rome. He did not function independent of Roman authority and an offense led to swift removal and replacement. Second, contrary to popular perception, we see that the high priest did not necessarily represent religious interests. Ananus was apparently insensitive or oblivious to the religious sensibilities of observant Jews. Third, we see that the prerogative of convening the Sanhedrin resided with the emperor or his representative. Ananus was removed from office for usurping Roman authority in this matter. We conclude from this episode that the first-century Sanhedrin was not a "standing committee" with oversight of religious concerns. It was an "ad hoc committee" of local prominent citizens summoned together by the procurator at the emperor's discretion to address the interests of the Roman system. Rivkin observes that Josephus does not use the term "Sanhedrin" for any permanent legislative body; for these he uses the term "*boule*." Rivkin argues that the pre-70 Sanhedrin did not possess a permanent religious or political status; it functioned as an adjunct to political authority.[16] Of course, this has significant implications for our understanding of the historical role of the Sanhedrin in the trial of Jesus. (If indeed there was one; Crossan thinks there was not, but his is a minority opinion.)

Given the diversity of early first-century Judaism, it stands to reason that Jews experienced Roman imperialism in different ways, even in Galilee and Judea. The Sadducean priestly families were most dependent on the Roman system; the high priests were appointed from among them, and their power was directly related to their ability to maneuver effectively under Roman authority. At the other end of the spectrum, the *sicarii* (the name means "assassins") were the active and, as the name implies, violent resisters.[17] Their motive was religious; they believed in the divine kingship of the God of Israel and regarded Roman rulers as godless imposters. The *sicarii* joined with the zealots in advocating resistance, which led to the Jewish War against Rome in 66 C.E. Scribes likely performed functions within the Roman bureaucracy that required the ability to read and write. Some Pharisees may have held these positions as well, but the Pharisees as a group were oriented toward Oral Torah and its observances as a way of Jewish life. They were neither active resisters of nor collaborators with Roman authority. Most Jews residing in Galilee and Judea were not aligned with any particular group. The people of the land were the most vulnerable to the oppressive nature of the Roman occupation. They experienced heavy tax burdens and confiscation of property that led to desperation and festering resentment toward Roman administration and any who prospered from it. The decades leading to the revolt against Rome provided a prime environment for prophetic voices with promises of divine deliverance and liberation, calling to mind earlier times of divine action in Israel's history.

The Gospels do not often speak explicitly about Roman imperialism either before or after the Jewish War, in the Jewish homeland or the Diaspora. But its presence is implicit, and we cannot understand the life and death of Jesus or the Gospel narratives apart from the presence of the Roman Empire. Rivkin describes the "mosaic of Judaism" within Rome's imperial grip and argues that the imperial system was responsible for Jesus' death.[18] Though we might resist blaming the system, thus relieving any individuals from responsibility, the images do help us keep in mind two historical certainties of the decades leading up to the Jewish War against Rome in the mid-60s: the diversity of Judaism and the direct effect of the Roman imperial system on Jewish life. These images, the "mosaic of Judaism" and "Rome's imperial grip," may help us overcome the most common occurrences of unintentional anti-Judaism in preaching and teaching on the Passion narrative.

Christians motivated to address the problem of anti-Judaism often distinguish between Jewish leaders and the people. The Jewish leaders were culpable, but not all Jews. Following the story line of the Gospels, the religious authorities tried Jesus, charged him with the trumped-up accusation of blasphemy, and turned him over to the Romans to be killed. The intent to distinguish among Jews and absolve all but religious authorities is admirable, but while this minimizes Jewish guilt to only a few, the anti-Judaism is nevertheless present.

A weekly feature in a local newspaper's "Faith and Values" section poses a question to which three clergy respond. Just prior to Holy Week, the question was: "Was Jesus crucified for getting involved in politics?" Two of the three responded in the affirmative. I agree with them, and I particularly liked the way they related Jesus' own political involvement with the suggestion that Christians ought to be involved in political processes for the sake of justice. But I was disappointed to see the caricature of Jewish religious leaders. For example, one respondent writes:

> Jesus' ministry challenged those who occupied the seats of power. He defied the religious authorities by opposing their interpretation of the laws and sacred texts, first given as a celebration of liberation and an invitation to joyful worship, but which they used to oppress and exclude. The radical distinction Jesus made between the emperor and God defied the power of the empire and threatened to undermine Roman rule. Jesus' death was most certainly political. He was killed for resisting religious and governmental authorities and the cruel peace their collusion produced.[19]

The caricature of religious authorities as abusive of both persons and religious traditions is an obvious distortion. More subtle is the charge of "collusion" between "religious and governmental authorities," as if they had equal power. It is true that only religious authorities are charged with oppression, exclusion, and collaborating with Roman powers, but there is no indication just exactly who these religious authorities are.

A second respondent asserts that "when Jesus loved the wrong people, he upset the status quo and broke the boundaries established by the religious authorities." And "Jesus was crucified by both religious and secular authorities, becoming our Christ."[20] And while I sense that the writer is speaking metaphorically here of Jesus' crucifixion by religious and secular authorities, it is likely to be heard as a description of historical truth.

I cite these responses to the question relating Jesus' death to first-century politics not because they represent the most blatant anti-Judaism but because they represent a common approach among those who presumably intend not to blame the Jews for Jesus' death. But simply substituting "religious authorities" for "the Jews" does nothing to diminish the anti-Judaism. The stereotypes of Judaism remain: exclusivism, an establishment with rigid boundaries, misinterpretation of their own Scriptures and traditions, and hostility toward Jesus. Also, naming the religious authorities implies that Jesus was executed at the initiation of Jews for religious reasons. This exaggerates the power of Jewish authorities and minimizes Roman interests in Jesus' death.

Also, blaming the religious authorities does not challenge our thinking about either the role of Jewish groups or of Roman authorities, or the relationship between the two with respect to Jesus' death. This tactic allows us to preserve the Gospel accounts quite literally without considering questions of historical context or reliability. In our best historical judgment, the Sanhedrin did not function in a religious capacity; it existed to serve the interests of Rome. Jews lived under Roman rule; some were harmed by the imperial system and some benefited by it. Whatever we say about the historical involvement of any Jews must take into account their place in the "web of the imperial system."

How then do we speak about Jewish groups named in the Passion narrative? In preaching and in teaching moments such as a brief response for a newspaper feature, we might avoid the repetition of the adjective "religious." An alternative is "Judean," as in "Judean authorities" or "leaders of the people" or simply "authorities." This avoids the constant reinforcement of religious, that is, Jewish, motives for Jesus' death. With respect to indigenous groups most closely connected with Roman interests, language that suggests independent power is misleading. Words like "collaboration" or "collusion" may be technically correct, but they are deceptive among Christians in a culture formed by the story of Jewish guilt. Such terms evoke disdain for the collaborators and overlook those who hold real power.

Why Did Roman Rulers Execute Jesus?

The Gospel accounts unequivocally state that the Roman procurator Pontius Pilate ordered Jesus' crucifixion. There is no reason to doubt that the Gospels report a historical fact at this point. This prompts us to ask why Roman rulers executed Jesus. What was the motive? This question distinguishes between later interpreters who found meaning in his death and resurrection and the historical events that led to his death. To answer the question, we must place Jesus' death within the wider context of Roman occupation in Galilee and Judea.

In the first place, Roman authorities needed little provocation to use crucifixion. This means of capital punishment was used extensively in the Jewish War, but descriptions of this cruel form of execution come from earlier times as well.[21] Josephus describes an incident involving the crucifixion of resisters from the lower classes who were trapped inside Jerusalem's walls and were caught when they tried to escape:

> They were accordingly scourged and subjected to torture of every description, before being killed, and then crucified opposite the walls. Titus commiserated their fate, five hundred or sometimes more being captured daily. . . . [Titus's] main reason for not stopping the crucifixions was the hope that the spectacle might perhaps induce the Jews to surrender, for fear that continued resistance would involve them in a similar fate. The soldiers out of rage and hatred amused themselves by nailing their prisoners in different postures; and so great was their number, that space could not be found for the crosses nor crosses for the bodies.[22]

Josephus makes a point to distinguish between the poorer classes and the rebels leading the resistance; he notes that the lower classes desired to desert the cause and return to their families but were caught between the rebels and the Roman soldiers. But these are the ones too numerous to count who were crucified, as Josephus tells it, to serve as an inducement to other Jews to surrender.

Granted, what Josephus describes here occurs within the context of war. Nevertheless, the use of crucifixion to discourage resistance was a frequent occurrence before the Jewish revolt. Jesus' death was not unusual in its cruelty; many suffered a similar fate in an even more ghastly fashion. Because death by crucifixion in occupied

Judea was all too common, it is not surprising that no early sources besides the Christian Gospels report his death. One of the criticisms of Gibson's *The Passion of the Christ* is that it conveys Jesus' crucifixion as an unusual historical event that commanded extraordinary attention.

The Gospels indicate that Jesus was crucified for political reasons. They report that a sign on the cross identified Jesus as "King of the Jews." This may provide a clue to Roman motives for getting rid of Jesus. The Gospels also tell us that Jesus began his ministry with the announcement of the coming of the kingdom of God: "The time is fulfilled, and the kingdom of God has come near; repent and believe in the good news" (Mark 1:15). Given the unrest of the mid-first century, the language of divine kingdoms and messianic deliverance would have been sufficient provocation to silence Jesus, just as Rome silenced other threats to Roman control.

Jesus' announcement of the advent of the kingdom of God had both political and religious currency. The kingdom of God meant the reign of the God of Israel, and it signaled an earthly reality. It evoked the hope and expectation of a divine rule characterized by justice and peace. God's kingdom implied an independent Israel and liberation from an oppressive foreign system of government. The kingdom of God called to mind prophetic voices advocating reversal of power, the mighty brought low, the lowly raised up, the hungry fed, preferential treatment of the poor. There is no reason to doubt that the announcement of the nearness of God's kingdom was central to Jesus' life and ministry, and that it was good news especially for those most vulnerable under the rule of Rome's emperor. But it would not be good news for Roman authorities dispatched to control Galilee and Judea. The interests of the imperial system were served by silencing those whose prophetic speech had the potential to draw crowds and incite resistance.

Jesus preached the nearness of God's reign. We do not know if Jesus intended to provoke Jews to resist Rome, though it seems unlikely that he was aligned with the *sicarii* or zealots or others who promoted active resistance. But he cannot have been oblivious to the powerful potential of his message, both for Jews longing for liberation and Rome's representatives determined to retain control.

When we place Jesus' death within the context of Roman imperialism, we conclude that Roman rulers ordered him crucified as a political subversive. He advocated a kingdom ruled by a God other than Caesar and posed a threat to incite others to resistance. Roman rulers did not need a trial nor did they need collaborators to justify crucifixions. They may have used local citizens to support certain actions, but there is sufficient evidence that this was not obligatory. An awareness of "the web of the imperial system" leads to a better understanding of the historical circumstances of Jesus' crucifixion.

The Historical Context of the Gospel Passion Narratives

The Gospel accounts of Jesus' Passion represent an interpretation of historical events. The diversity of first-century Judaism and the presence of Roman imperialism are relevant contextual clues for reading the Gospel Passion narratives. They are important in reconstructing the historical circumstances surrounding Jesus' death. But the Gospels were written after the revolt against Rome and in the Diaspora. (Matthew is the exception, perhaps written in Galilee.) A context different from pre-70 Judea affects how we define the diversity of Judaism and Jewish experience of Roman imperialism.

In the Diaspora, the Jewish experience of imperialism varied. Certainly there was a wide disparity between those who suffered through Roman occupation in Judea and those who lived in peaceful coexistence with their neighbors far from Jerusalem. Judaism itself underwent a dramatic shift with the devastation of Jerusalem and the destruction of the Temple. This marked the end of priestly families as Temple functionaries; it also decimated the advocates for revolt against Rome and the establishment of an independent Israel, a kingdom under God's reign. We cannot overestimate the symbolic impact of the loss of the Temple. This above all marks the end of biblical Judaism. The exile from land and place, the termination of sacrificial cult and its priestly caretakers, and the location of divine presence belonged to Israel's biblical rituals and identity. In the wake of the loss, a process of identity formation characterized Judaism in its diversity. The term "formative Judaism" is an apt description of this period in the last decades of the first century.

Pharisaism, already a presence in the Diaspora, survived as the leading viable form of Judaism. The Pharisees had already successfully begun a reformation within Judaism with the development of the Oral Torah, in itself a shift from the exclusive authority of Written

Torah and biblical traditions. The orientation toward the sanctity of time and the observance of the sacred in the ordinary aspects of daily life translated well to Diaspora situations. The synagogue emerged as a key institution for the reformation of Judaism.

The Gospel communities were formed in the belief that Jesus was God's anointed king and that God raised Jesus from the dead. They applied the Pharisaic belief in resurrection to Jesus: though he has died yet he lives. They grounded their definition of Jewish identity in the prophetic promises of God to Israel and looked to God's future in the return of Jesus the Messiah/Christ. Their message was also adaptable to a post-Temple Diaspora setting, and missionaries were eager to spread the word. From the perspective of the Gospel communities, the Pharisees were the primary competition in defining Judaism after the destruction of the Temple.

We discussed the diversity of early Judaism in chapter 1, "The Gospels as Jewish Literature." The focus here is on the Gospels' Passion narratives within the context of formative Judaism in the late first century and within the broader context of the Roman Empire. And so we consider how these factors shape the Gospels' interpretation of a historical event.

A favorite seminary professor used to say that the Bible was written "from faith for faith."[23] That is certainly true of the Gospel Passion narratives. The Gospels tell the story of Jesus through the lens of resurrection faith. The early followers of Jesus believed that God raised Jesus from the dead. Jesus' death leads to his resurrection, the means through which God overcomes the power of death and sin. Because it is by God's divine purpose that Jesus was raised from the dead, then it must be in continuity with Israel's sacred story. The narrative of Jesus' Passion is told as the fulfillment of the Scriptures. (In chapter 2, "Supersessionism," we observed that prophecy-fulfillment interpretations of Scripture work backward, from the experience of an event back to a biblical precedent.) The references to Isaiah's suffering servant are a good example. As we noted above, Crossan argues that "prophecy historicized" provides the dominant structure for the Passion narrative.[24] Regardless of the extent that prophecy contributes to the telling of the story, the Gospel narratives make their case for the divine meaning of Jesus' death on a cross from Israel's Scriptures.

The Gospel narratives were written also to serve the interests of apologetics. The narrative contains a judgment against those who did not agree with the Gospel communities' interpretation of God's divine presence in Jesus' suffering, death, and resurrection. In the years following 70 C.E. there were Jews who believed Jesus was God's Messiah whom God resurrected, and more who did not. From the perspective of the Gospel writers, the identity of Jesus as God's Messiah was the defining moment in Israel's history and determined the future of God with Israel. The account of his suffering and death is told as an intra-Jewish conflict, and it reflects the realities of formative Judaism after 70 more than before 70. Antagonists within the narrative represent post-70 rivals. The Gospel Passion narratives exaggerate the roles of religious leaders and religious themes, such as a hastily convened Sanhedrin trial by night and trumped-up religious motives for Jesus' death. The context of the Gospel communities within post-70 Judaism shapes the final form of the Passion narratives in the Gospels. That does not mean that we must conclude that there was no trial nor that there were no opponents who did not object to Jesus' death, but neither does it mean that the Gospels report events as they actually happened. Whatever the kernel of historicity, these aspects of the narratives belong to the world of formative Judaism before the schism between Judaism and Christianity.

The Gospels amplify religious conflict in the Passion narratives and diminish Roman responsibility for Jesus' death. Primary sources concur that Pilate was notoriously cruel toward his subjects in Judea. The portrayal of Pilate in the Gospel Passion narratives is remarkably benign by comparison. The Gospel accounts clearly shift the blame from Pilate to the Jewish leaders. This move is prudent. In light of the recent revolt and considering the dominant culture, it is not surprising the Gospel writers downplay Roman culpability and emphasize religious motives for Jesus' death. Also, Rome's motives for Jesus' death were no longer relevant. The kingdom of God did not carry the same political potency after the war. We see in the Gospels some tendencies to spiritualize the kingdom toward an otherworldly reality. Some of the ambiguities concerning the kingdom of God in the Gospels are due to the presence of both history remembered and history interpreted in light of later contexts.

Preaching
during Holy Week

Confronting the historical truth of the Passion narrative opens different possibilities for preaching. For example, when we consider the historical reasons for Jesus' death, we necessarily connect the circumstances of his death with his life. Jesus' announcement of the nearness of God's kingdom led to his death. Traditional Christian theology has emphasized Jesus' purpose in terms of his death. "He came to die for us" is a common expression of Jesus' purpose in the divine plan. In *Constantine's Sword*, James Carroll sums up a key point of Peter Abelard's theology (1072–1142): "Thus Jesus did not come to die, but to live as a human being, to embrace the human condition, which includes death. Death here is a moment, not a purpose, a part of the life story, not the meaning of it."[25] Jesus proclaimed the coming of God's reign and he lived as if it were a present reality, aligning with the poor and others regardless of the risk. He inspired others and consequently threatened the ruling order of his world. This perspective lends itself very well to preaching, and from it, it is easy to avoid typical anti-Judaism.

The following is a Good Friday sermon that emerges from the observation that the way Jesus lived caused his death. Here I explore the ordinary and extraordinary in Jesus' suffering and death and their meaning in our own lives:[26]

This week's Newsweek *magazine features several articles on the Middle East, on the survival of Israel and the continuing violence on the part of Israeli occupiers and Palestinian terrorists. Hadas Haipak, an Israeli teenager, was quoted as saying, "Maybe we are going to learn to get along with all the violence. It will become part of us." Another observed that the fact of violence permeates daily life, not least of all because the suicide bombers choose targets which are ordinary—a commuter bus, a pizzeria, a shopping mall, a disco, a bat mitzvah, the stuff of the ordinary, routine.*

On 9/11, we were horrified by the attack on office buildings when people were just beginning an ordinary workday, devastated by the loss of innocent life to another kind of suicide bomber. Analysts equated the attack to Pearl Harbor. Our friends around the world expressed sympathy, shared our outrage. At the same time, there were voices that reminded us we had just experienced what others live with on a daily basis—the threat of terrorism.

The narrative of Jesus' trial and death with all of its details convey an extraordinary event: arrest, mock trial, handing Jesus over to Pilate the Roman procurator, the debate about whom to release, the crucifixion of Jesus with two others, the mocking of the guards. But the facts of history, of life under Roman occupation, yield a somewhat different picture. Crucifixions were very ordinary, there being accounts of hundreds at a time. No trial, fair or otherwise, no conversation with accusers, or with the crowds. Crucifixions were a mechanism of crowd control. The cruel execution of political subversives, anyone accused of a crime, guilty or not, was ordinary, violence something one learned to get along with, a part of how things were.

It is a witness to the best of the human spirit, though, to refuse to allow violence, particularly innocent suffering and death, to become ordinary. The Arab Summit of peace talks are an attempt to normalize relations, so that neither Palestinian nor Israeli children will become resigned to violence; something mundane that they will learn to get along with. And, though many of us are critical of the tactics of our war on terrorism, the rejection of the threat of terrorism as something that we must become accustomed to is necessary. We must refuse to allow innocent suffering and death to become somehow ordinary.

It is a witness to faith that the early followers of Jesus perceived the extraordinary in the ordinary violence of Roman occupiers. They could have quite easily concluded that they had been wrong about Jesus, their friend, healer, teacher, the one who proclaimed justice in his preaching of the coming of God's kingdom (no wonder the defenders of the imperial system killed him—no room for competing kingdoms here). But they were convinced that in the presence of this one there was the God of their ancestors, God of Israel, God with us. And so they sought understanding, meaning—out of their tradition, their Scriptures, their experience.

And so they—and we—see in Jesus' death the extraordinary. The willingness to lay down one's life for others. A favorite seminary teacher of mine said, when speaking of the passion of Jesus, "it matters that Jesus did not go kicking and screaming to the cross."[27] I pondered those words, which seemed at first shocking to me, not quite sure what he meant. But I finally got it. It matters that Jesus is not a victim. He made a willing sacrifice, choosing to live fully at one with God. That, of course, the powers of the world cannot bear.

The cross, a very ordinary means of capital punishment, is transformed into a symbol of the willingness to sacrifice for the sake of others. Symbol of life, in that we do not understand his death apart from his resurrection. Symbol of hope, that this life is not all there is. Symbol of Christian identity, for the narrative of Jesus' passion, his death, and resurrection is our story, the one that tells the truth about God. Jesus becomes the human face of God. Jesus' suffering and death has for the Christian extraordinary significance, for it is how we make sense of our own experiences of suffering and death. Certainly people have different ways of making meaning of suffering, indeed the Bible has different ways of making meaning, of responding, to suffering.

We find in Jesus' suffering and death on the cross a companion in our own suffering. Standing at the foot of the cross we know that suffering is not good, but that good can come of it. And we find here permission to cry out, "My God why have you abandoned me?" We see in Jesus' suffering inspiration to take a stand for the sake of justice whatever the cost. We are able, because of the cross, to make hard choices, life-and-death choices, trusting in the promise that this life is not all there is, for the cross is not only about suffering and death, it is about resurrection and new life.

It was twenty-two years ago this month that Archbishop Oscar Romero was assassinated in San Salvador while celebrating Mass. I often think of him as a modern example of a life lived fully for the sake of God's kingdom, knowing that inevitably it would lead to his death. And, like Jesus, living with the reality that he would not see God's kingdom come to fruition in his own life. And, like Moses before him, who led people to the promised land but did not himself enter it. In a homily given not long before his death, Romero spoke of taking the long view of our vocation with respect to God's kingdom:

"It helps now and then to step back and take the long view. The kingdom is not only beyond our efforts; it is beyond our vision. We accomplish in our lifetime only a tiny fraction of the magnificent enterprise that is God's work. Nothing we do is complete, which is another way of saying that the kingdom always lies beyond us. No statement says all that could be said. No prayer fully expresses our faith. No confession brings perfection. No pastoral visit brings wholeness. No pro-

gram accomplishes the church's mission. No set of goals and objectives includes everything. This is what we are about. We plant seeds that one day will grow. We water the seeds already planted, knowing that they hold future promise. We lay foundations that will need further development. We provide yeast that produces effects beyond our capabilities. We cannot do everything and there is a sense of liberation in realizing that. This enables us to do something, and to do it very well. It may be incomplete, but it is a beginning, a step along the way, an opportunity for God's grace to enter and do the rest. We may never see the end results, but that is the difference between the master builder and the work. We are workers, not builders, ministers, not messiahs. We are prophets of a future not our own."[28]

Romero's homily tells the extraordinary truth, that from the perspective of the cross, the ordinary offerings of our lives are blessed with meaning in the larger scope of bringing God's kingdom, which is to say God's justice, to fruition. Romero's life and death bears witness to the cross as a symbol of hope and of life beyond our own.

Hannah Arendt, a victim of the Holocaust, claimed that the ultimate horror of human evil is seen not in the spectacular, a sudden and shocking evil. The ultimate horror of human evil is when it becomes an ordinary, everyday, ongoing event. She referred to it as "the banality of evil."[29] A subtext of the narrative of Jesus' suffering and death is the rejection of the banality of evil. In the midst of violence as ordinary, crucifixions too frequent and numerous to mention, the followers of Jesus told the story of a cruel death which had and has cosmic meaning, filled with divine purpose—suffering and death that was redeemed by God in the resurrection.

On Good Friday 2002, it is that subtext that carries extra significance for us, for our world. At the foot of the cross this year, may we find renewed resolve to resist the banality of evil. So that next year, no child, Israeli or Palestinian or in New York or Chicago or on the continent of Africa will conclude that maybe we are going to learn to get along with all the violence. It will become part of us.

I confess that I have used the concept of this sermon more than once, so I know that it is adaptable to different situations. It seems that violence and the banality of evil have not yet been conquered.

Whether the historical circumstances of Jesus' death are an integral part of a sermon's theme or not, most sermons could easily include at least a brief mention of historical realities, such as the use of crucifixion as a frequently used means of capital punishment, or effects of Roman imperialism. One can also employ positive references to modern Jewish leaders and Jewish life to counter the negative portrayals of Jews in the Gospel narratives. Since Holy Week and Passover usually coincide, reflections on Jewish life are then more prominent in the news than at other times and therefore readily accessible to draw upon for sermon illustrations.

Another strategy for Holy Week preaching is to lift up Passover themes. The narratives concur that Jesus' death occurred at Passover. Jesus' death as liberation from bondage echoes the deliverance from the bondage of slavery. The parallels between Passover and Easter are clearly evident. This approach has the advantage of connecting with contemporary Jewish observance and validating Judaism, particularly in a season when Christians have notoriously harmed Jews. Presbyterian pastor Barbara Anderson linked Passover and Easter in an Easter sermon. She began by citing the problem of the historicity of biblical accounts of events that are central to the celebration of Passover and Easter:

> On Friday, the Los Angeles Times *ran an article on page one dealing with the story we read from Exodus. Judaism has been celebrating Passover this week, the season when it remembers and celebrates God's liberation of the Hebrews from slavery in Egypt. So it was front-page news when a rabbi in Westwood told a congregation that for nearly two decades, scholars and archeologists have grown increasingly doubtful that the Israelites were really slaves in Egypt, wandered in the desert for 40 years, or conquered Canaan in the way their Bible and ours say it happened.*
>
> *Judaism is now invited to deal with the ramifications of a question raised half a century ago by the great Christian theologian, Rudolf Bultmann, regarding the resurrection. The question is: If you had been there with a camera, could you have taken a picture of the slaves leaving Egypt and does it matter if the answer is really "no"? As spiritual descendants through Jesus Christ of those who consider God's liberation of them from slavery to be the foundational event of their faith, it is a fascinating question for us to ponder as well.*
>
> *This morning we remember that Exodus and Easter are linked together not only because people question their historical factuality, but*

because they are the same story, two sides of the same coin, two varia-
tions on the same theme, Easter a dramatic remake of an earlier ver-
sion. They speak of the truths of God we know already in life: that God
leads each of us from slavery into freedom, from death into life. God
conquers suffering, injustice, loneliness, lies and evil with life and jus-
tice, love and truth and good. God has the power to break us free from
whatever holds us captive and bring us into the Promised Land.[30]

Her sermon continues by exploring the exodus metaphor with examples of liberation in individual lives and in our world, constantly linking Exodus and Easter. She returns to her original question of historicity:

Exodus and Easter. They are more than words on a page or histori-
cal facts that may sometime be disproved by archeological evidence.
Exodus and Easter. They are eternal Truth that has reached into the
prisons of our life and our world, and gives us hope of freedom.

Do I believe that Jesus Christ was raised from the dead on Easter
morning? Do I believe in the resurrection? Absolutely, I do. I can no
more explain exactly what happened on that first Easter than has any-
one else through the centuries, including the Gospel writers, who each
give a different story, but I know its truth.[31]

What is particularly effective in this sermon is that the fundamental truth of the foundational narratives of Judaism and Christianity form the theme of the sermon, which is God as liberator. The stories differ but they tell the same truth. And I also appreciate that the question of historicity is raised but in a nonthreatening way. The Easter sermon does not present the same difficulties with anti-Judaism that Good Friday does, but it offers a wonderful opportunity to lift up what Jews and Christians have in common.

Maundy Thursday provides another opportunity to focus on Passover. The Episcopal lectionary assigns the Lukan account of the Last Supper as an alternative to the selection from John. According to Luke (and Mark and Matthew) the Last Supper is a Passover seder, so the narrative lends itself to preaching on common Jewish and Christian topics. I have seized the opportunity in several homilies. The following are excerpts from a sermon on Passover remembering:

It is Passover remembering that we see in Luke's narrative of Jesus' Passover seder with his disciples. A careful reading indicates this remembering, a layering of past, present, and future. What the God of Israel has done, is doing, will accomplish shapes the remembering. Here, Jesus is at the center. Jesus presides at this seder at which the story of God's deliverance from Egypt was told, and Jesus will preside at the table in God's kingdom. Jesus presides at the seder but does not participate in it; he does not eat. He is our Passover, the One through whom God accomplishes liberation for us.

After citing hope for liberation in current affairs, I turn to the future:

Passover remembering is eschatological remembering. Remembering which relates to the future, most specifically God's future. Passover remembering, Eucharistic remembering, is an act of faith, confident that time, past, present, and future, belongs to God. The God of Israel we have known, liberator, redeemer, peacemaker, savior, is the One who is and will be.

The Passover seder that Jews observe this week traditionally concludes: Next year in Jerusalem. That is eschatological remembering. Next year when we gather for this seder may God's liberation from slavery find its fulfillment when the cycle of terror and retaliation is broken. Do this in remembrance of me. Our act of remembrance, whenever we do this, is oriented toward the future, when at last betrayal, suffering, and death will end and neither will there be war anymore.

And back to the present:

But now we are here, conflicted in the tenuousness of human decision. Aware of our finitude, easily distracted, like the disciples, from our commitments and loyalty, yet determined to be faithful. We might despair, except for our remembering. Jesus said, "Do this in remembrance of me." We do, remembering what God has done, remembering our confident hope in God's future, claiming the transforming presence of God in Christ even in the messy tangle of the present moment.[32]

The Passion narrative contains challenges for the preacher not present on Maundy Thursday and Easter with respect to anti-Judaism. Passion Sunday and Good Friday require the preacher to counter the weight of traditional anti-Judaism. Maundy Thursday and Easter offer opportunities during Holy Week to emphasize commonalities between Jews and Christians apart from the burden of damage control.

Our focus here is on preaching, but preaching alone cannot overpower the anti-Judaism we hear in the Passion narratives. A public reading of any one of the Gospel accounts reinforces in our ears the Jewish rejection of Jesus. Throughout history the Passion play presented the most powerful indictment against the Jews. These became popular in the medieval era, and the visual effect of Jewish characters dressed in black with pointed black hats, cast as evil plotters to execute Jesus, incited Christians to attack Jews. The well-known Oberammergau Passion Play, still produced every decade, was but one example of portraying Jews as "Christ-killers." Gibson's *The Passion of the Christ* is a modern version of the Passion play. The Passion play is so closely associated with persecution of Jews it is no wonder that many Jews feared the potential effect of the popular movie. Fortunately, there are many resources available to guide Christian leaders who not only preach but also plan liturgy and education forums. The Vatican has endorsed guidelines for Passion plays, and the Oberammergau play responded to criticisms in their most recent production.[33] There are also several Passion narrative readings created for liturgical use and for teaching that address the problem of reinforcing anti-Judaism.[34]

Hymns are a strong influence in reinforcing traditional views, and they may be the most difficult to change. We are likely attached to singing the same ones during Holy Week each year. But where there are opportunities to introduce new hymns or even responsive readings, Brian Wren's *Piece Together Praise* is an excellent resource. Imagine a Holy Week worship service that includes this:

> God, thank you for the Jews.
>> Redeem your church's ancient crime.
> Believing Christ had come,
>> we cursed them as forever wrong,
> through centuries of hate
> that paved the devil's way

to Auschwitz, and the Holocaust.
How could your Christians be so blind?
 Kyrie eleison!
 Christe eleison!
 Kyrie eleison!

God, thank you for the Jews.
 Their sorrow shows our common sin.
With sad, demonic pride,
 we fill our world with sheep and goats,
and feed our self-esteem
by doing others down,
applauding "us" and cursing "them,"
Like crowds who mock the crucified.
 Kyrie eleison!
 Christe eleison!
 Kyrie eleison!

God, thank you for the Jews.
 We celebrate their living faith.
Help us, who long to mend
 our ancient parting of the ways,
to recognize their claim,
and utter Jesus' name,
not in polemic, but in praise,
till all our hopes are made complete.
 Hallelujah!
 Amen!*

Music, poetry and drama are powerful means of influencing faith. This presents a challenge during Holy Week; it also provides opportunity for transformation.

* * *

The suffering, death, and resurrection of Jesus is the identity-defining story of Christianity. Belief in God's victory over sin and

*Words by Brian Wren. © 1986, 1996 Hope Publishing Co., Carol Stream, IL 60188. All rights reserved. Used by permission.

death through Christ's resurrection is fundamental to Christian faith. That this story has been used as a weapon against Jews is the church's sin. It is time to repent and learn to tell the story without contempt for Judaism.

Conclusion

ON SEVERAL OCCASIONS, well-known preacher Barbara Brown Taylor has written of her growing awareness of anti-Judaism in her sermons. She describes the experience of receiving a letter from someone who had heard several sermons on tape. He spoke well of her sermons, but he added:

> Still, when I listened to the earlier set of tapes, there were times when I cringed to hear echoes of the old "teaching of contempt." It seemed like you looked underneath the surface of everyone in the gospel stories, showing complex motivations and spiritual struggles—yet your portrayal of Jesus' opponents and the Pharisees seemed one-dimensional and lacking in sympathy.

Taylor was stunned at the criticism: "Me? Engaged in the teaching of contempt?" But when she looked at the sermons in question, she was taken aback that he was right:

> I had helped Jesus make his case by nailing the Pharisees as self-righteous prigs. Reducing them to cardboard cutouts of everything I found despicable in religious people, I was not only able to blow them away handily. I was also able to congratulate myself for doing so.
>
> All these years later, it is clear that I did Jesus no favors by lampooning his opponents. His ministry involved engaging real people with real concerns, not defeating cartoon characters. It is even clearer that I maligned observant Jews everywhere by painting those who love Torah with the same old scorn-full brush.[1]

She followed up the recognition of "preaching contempt" in her sermons by reflecting on how it had happened:

> Fourteen years ago, I believed that the New Testament told me the whole truth about Pharisaic Judaism. Nothing in my church or seminary education led me to believe otherwise. None of the commentaries I used to prepare my sermons challenged the traditional story of Christian origins.

And she noted what changed her thinking:

> I do not remember whether it was Jack Spong or Marcus Borg who first raised serious questions about that story for me, but they led me to Jewish teachers such as Jacob Neusner and Paula Fredriksen (as well as Christian ones such as E. P. Sanders and Mary Boys), who have enriched my reading of the New Testament by helping me recognize the nature of its polemics.
>
> Simply to find those teachers changed the way I preached about Torah, Talmud and Judaism. Then a man in my congregation married a Jewish woman who sometimes came with him to church. When she did, I heard the slurs in familiar passages. I tasted the razor blades in beloved hymns. Before long, she had changed my sermons even when she was not there. If what I said did not sound like good news to her, I decided, then it was not the gospel of Jesus Christ.[2]

Barbara Brown Taylor is one of the most prominent preachers in America today, a sought-after speaker, teacher, and author. I cite her story here to illustrate a common occurrence among preachers as well as summarize the aims of this book. As the title suggests, I address preachers who do not intentionally malign Judaism but who nevertheless unwittingly repeat familiar anti-Jewish stereotypes in sermons, just as Taylor had done before someone pointed it out to her. My intent in this book is to bring about that moment of awareness and the ensuing questions: Why does this happen? How does it change?

There are several reasons the preaching of contempt continues, and Taylor alludes to them. Anti-Judaism is woven into the conventional history and theology of Christian origin and traditional interpretations of the Scriptures. We learn it in our earliest formation as Christians. It is so familiar we do not hear it or recognize it. The Gospel narratives are the most common source for biblical preaching and, when read apart from their historical contexts, reinforce caricatures of Judaism. Commentaries and homiletical resources typically do not provide insight or correctives. Seminary curriculums rarely offer a consistent critique of the problem or the tools to relate theory and practice.

Taylor refers to a few scholars who helped her see the teaching of contempt and thus to correct misrepresentations of Judaism in her preaching. My purpose is to provide a useful resource not only for illuminating the problem but also proposing useful strategies for overcoming conventional anti-Judaism.

A grasp of the diversity of first-century Judaism is essential to counter the Christian construction of an inferior Judaism created to serve the purposes of Christian supersessionism. An understanding of first-century Judaism puts Newer Testament polemics in context. I argue that the Gospels were Jewish literature written before the schism between Judaism and Christianity. They reflect late first-century intra-Jewish controversies. The Gospel writers did not describe Judaism from the perspective of Christian outsiders. This observation potentially diminishes the "us vs. them" approach of much preaching. Acquaintance with Judaism on its own terms also leads to a revision of the conventional story of the origin of Christianity. Overcoming unintended anti-Judaism requires the preacher to proclaim the gospel on its own terms without depending on an inferior "other" to make it attractive. Preachers can trust that the good news of Jesus Christ is compelling on its own terms.

Taylor observes the effect of having a Jewish presence in her congregation, observing that this changes her sermons whether the person is there or not. A strong motive to avoid negative portrayals of Jews is the potential to hurt people. The fact is that we never know for sure who will hear our sermons. I suggest that preachers routinely imagine how a sermon might sound to Jewish ears. It is a good way to check unintended anti-Judaism that might be missed because of its familiarity.

In telling her story, Barbara Brown Taylor illustrates effectively the point that overcoming unintended anti-Judaism has far-reaching consequences. It does not end with correcting misrepresentations of Judaism. It extends to the core of the Gospel. My own passion for eradicating anti-Judaism is grounded in the conviction that it is antithetical to the Gospel. Ultimately that is what is at stake—the good news of God in Jesus Christ we proclaim in sermons week and after week. In the gospel, there is no room for preaching contempt.

Notes

Introduction

1. I am not critical of the use of lectionaries. In my tradition, we follow the lectionary in the Episcopal Book of Common Prayer or the Revised Common Lectionary Episcopal Edition, and I am committed to this custom. My observations here are to call attention to the ways the lectionary propers assert certain interpretations of biblical texts.

2. I believe that both modern Judaism and Christianity are second-century developments, each emerging out of first-century Judaism. It is possible that Pharisaism can be regarded as the parent of both Rabbinic Judaism and Christianity!

3. John Dominic Crossan, *Who Killed Jesus? Exposing the Roots of Anti-Semitism in the Gospel Story of the Death of Jesus* (San Francisco: HarperSanFrancisco, 1995), 32.

4. James Carroll, *Constantine's Sword: The Church and the Jews, a History* (New York: Houghton Mifflin, 2001).

5. John T. Pawlikowski, *Christ in the Light of Christian-Jewish Dialogue,* Studies in Judaism and Christianity (New York: Paulist, 1982), and Paul M. Van Buren, *A Theology of the Jewish-Christian Reality* (San Francisco: Harper & Row, 1987) are among the first systematic theologies that take seriously the issue of Christian anti-Judaism.

6. See, for example, Daniel Boyarin, *A Radical Jew: Paul and the Politics of Identity,* Contraversions 1 (Berkeley: University of California Press, 1994); Richard B. Hays, *Echoes of Scripture in the Letters of Paul* (New Haven: Yale University Press, 1989); Calvin J. Roetzel, *Paul: The Man and the Myth* (Minneapolis: Fortress Press, 1999); Krister Stendahl, *Paul among Jews and Gentiles and Other Essays* (Philadelphia: Fortress Press, 1976). For scholarship on the Gospels, see, for example, Donald H. Juel, *The Gospel*

of Mark, Interpreting Biblical Texts (Nashville: Abingdon, 1999); J. Andrew Overman, *Church and Community in Crisis: The Gospel according to Matthew* (Valley Forge, Pa.: Trinity Press International, 1996); Anthony J. Saldarini, *Matthew's Christian-Jewish Community,* Chicago Studies in the History of Judaism (Chicago: University of Chicago Press, 1994). For several Lukan scholars who place the writer of Luke-Acts within the context of first-century Judaism, see Joseph B. Tyson, *Luke, Judaism, and the Scholars: Critical Approaches to Luke-Acts* (Columbia: University of South Carolina Press, 1999); *Luke-Acts and the Jewish People: Eight Critical Perspectives,* ed. Joseph B. Tyson (Minneapolis: Augsburg, 1988). For Johannine studies, see *Anti-Judaism and the Fourth Gospel,* ed. Reimund Bieringer, et al. (Louisville: Westminster John Knox, 2001).

7. See Ronald J. Allen and Clark M. Williamson, *Interpreting Difficult Texts: Anti-Judaism and Christian Preaching* (Philadelphia: Trinity Press International, 1989).

8. The classroom example was offered in a roundtable discussion at Luther Seminary, St. Paul, Minn., 1998. Amy-Jill Levine is the E. Rhodes and Leona B. Carpenter Professor of New Testament Studies in the Vanderbilt University Divinity School and Graduate Department of Religion.

9. See *Anti-Judaism and the Fourth Gospel,* ed. Reimund Bieringer, et al., for a range of perspectives.

1. The Gospels as Jewish Literature

1. Early Judaism replaces the term "late Judaism" among Christian scholars. Early Judaism is used widely in scholarship, Christian and non-Christian, to designate Judaism in approximately the second century B.C.E. through the second C.E. Early Judaism includes the first century C.E.

2. *Jubilees,* in *The Apocryphal Old Testament,* ed. H. F. D. Sparks, trans. R. H. Charles, rev. C. Rabin (Oxford: Clarendon, 1984).

3. Josephus, *Jewish Antiquities,* trans. H. St. J. Thackeray, Loeb Classical Library (Cambridge, Mass.: Harvard University Press, 1976).

4. *Philo of Alexandria,* trans. F. H. Colson and G. H. Whitaker, Loeb Classical Library (Cambridge, Mass.: Harvard University Press, 1929–1962). In *Virtutibus* 20.103–14, Philo claims that the Torah commands Jews to welcome proselytes; according to *De Specialibus Legibus* 1.9.52, the Torah requires Jews to show extraordinary goodwill toward proselytes. In *Legation and Gaium* 31.211, Philo implies that Jews ought to welcome proselytes as equals.

5. See Matt. 23:15. It appears from this passage that the Matthean community competed with the Pharisees for followers and recognition.

6. Menahem Stern, "The Jews in Greek and Latin Literature," in *The Jewish People in the First Century: Historical Geography, Political History, Social, Cultural and Religious Life and Institutions.* ed. Shmuel Safrai and Menahem Stern, 2 vols., Compendia Rerum Iudaicarum ad Novum Testamentum (Fortress Press: Philadelphia, 1976), 2:1157.

7. See Shaye J. D. Cohen, "Crossing the Boundary and Becoming a Jew," *Harvard Theological Review* 82 (1989): 13–33. Reprinted in *The Beginnings of Jewishness: Boundaries, Varieties, Uncertainties,* Hellenistic Culture and Society (Berkeley: University of California Press, 1999).

8. See, for example, 13:16. See also the description of Cornelius in 10:1-2. Inscriptions of synagogue members also include references to "God-fearers."

9. Obviously this applies to Jewish males only and not to Jewish women. The literature of the period represents a predominantly male perspective.

10. *Mishnah* literally means "teaching."

11. *Halacha* means "law," but it derives from the verb meaning "to walk" or "go forth" and, like *Torah,* has the connotation of "way of life."

12. Mark 2:23-27 and parallels Matt. 12:1-8 and Luke 6:1-5; Mark 3:1-6 and parallels Matt. 12:9-14 and Luke 6:6-11; Luke 13:10-17 and 14:1-6.

13. Stern, "The Jews in Greek and Latin Literature," 2:1101–57.

14. Josephus, *Letter of Aristeas,* trans. R. J. H. Shutt, in *The Old Testament Pseudepigrapha,* vol. 1, *The Old Testament Pseudepigrapha,* ed. James H. Charlesworth, 2 vols. (Garden City, N.Y.: Doubleday, 1985), 2:182–86.

15. Gary Porton, *Goyim: Gentiles and Israelites in Mishnah-Tosefta* (Atlanta: Scholars, 1988), 251.

16. Richard B. Hays, in the commentary on Gal. 2:11-21 in the *HarperCollins Study Bible,* is right in stating that Jewish Law did not prohibit eating with Gentiles. He suggests that the vacillation on the part of Cephas and Barnabas "shows that the Jerusalem agreement (2:7-10) had failed to address the problem of table fellowship." *HarperCollins Study Bible: New Revised Standard Version, with the Apocryphal/Deuterocanonical Books,* ed. Wayne A. Meeks (New York: HarperCollins, 1993), s.v. Galatians.

17. See Neh. 8:1-8. Scholars date the writing of Nehemiah in the mid-fifth century B.C.E.

18. What we call Chronicles is in the Jewish Bible called *divrei hayamim,* literally, "words of the days."

19. See the midrashim of the early centuries of the Common Era such as *Mechilta,* the commentaries on Exodus (there are two of them), *Sifra,* on Leviticus, and *Sifre,* on Deuteronomy.

20. I will discuss the Fourth Gospel in chapter 4, because of the particular issues related to that Gospel. I note here, however, that John, too, begins with an allusion to the Scriptures: "In the beginning. . . ."

21. See note 1 in the introduction. The citation is not exactly the same as it appears in Isaiah.

22. The NRSV takes the two questions as a *hendiadys*, translating the second question, "What do you read there?" I prefer the RSV translation. It is more literal and preserves the meaning that the second question implies not reading but *interpreting* what is read.

23. I concur with mainstream scholarship in regarding the polemic against the Pharisees as belonging to the time the Gospel was written, not the time of Jesus.

24. See, for example, 16:1-5; 21:17-26; 22:3; 23:1-5; 23:6.

25. See the account of the Jerusalem Council in Acts 15. The Apostolic Decree (vv. 19-21 and repeated in 15:29 and 21:25) confirms the compromise. Gentiles need not be circumcised but are expected to observe dietary laws, sexual purity customs, and, implied, Sabbath customs.

26. I attribute Paul's inclusion of Gentiles apart from Torah observance to his own historical context and his view of the imminence of the parousia, not his personal aversion to the Law. Paul was pragmatic; there was not sufficient time to engage in a Gentile mission that included enculturation as a Torah observant member of Israel.

27. I am not questioning the doctrine; I observe only that it was not an issue in the Synoptic Gospels. This doctrine evolved over the early centuries of Christian history. The Council at Nicea in the early fourth century struggled to define the two natures of Jesus, a good indication that the matter was not resolved before then.

2. Supersessionism

1. Robert Jenson, "Toward a Christian Theology of Judaism," *Jews and Christians: People of God*, ed. Carl Braaten and Robert Jenson (Grand Rapids, Mich.: Eerdmans, 2003), 6.

2. Krister Stendahl, "Anti-Judaism and the New Testament," *Explorations* 7, no. 2 (1993): 7. Stendahl poses this question, a rhetorical one.

3. In current conversations, several argue for an even later date for separate identities.

4. R. P. C. Hanson, ed. and trans., *Justin Martyr's Dialogue with Trypho, a Jew* (New York: Associated Press, 1964).

5. See "Medieval Handbook: Saint John Chrysostom: Eight Homilies Against the Jews," http://www.fordham.edu/halsall/source/chrysostom -jews6.html (accessed October 21, 2005).

6. Fredrick C. Holmgren, *The Old Testament and the Significance of Jesus: Embracing Change—Maintaining Christian Identity* (Grand Rapids, Mich.: Eerdmans, 1999), 41.

7. Ibid.

8. Sermon delivered on the Fourth Sunday in Advent, St. Clement's Episcopal Church, St. Paul, Minn., December 24, 1995.

9. We do need to be careful of reading later rabbinic literature back into the first century, but the question of motives is part of New Testament polemic and later Christian projection.

10. Ronald J. Allen and Clark M. Williamson, *Preaching the Gospels without Blaming the Jews: A Lectionary Commentary* (Louisville: Westminster John Knox, 2004), 19.

11. Marianne Edgar Budde, homily delivered on Ash Wednesday, St. John the Baptist Episcopal Church, Minneapolis, Minn., February 9, 2005.

12. Sermon delivered on the Third Sunday of Lent, St. Clement's Episcopal Church, St. Paul, Minn., March 6, 1988.

13. Gerd Theissen and Dagmar Winter, *The Quest for the Plausible Jesus: The Question of Criteria*, trans. Eugene Boring (Louisville: Westminster John Knox, 2002), 1.

14. Karl Theodor Keim, *Geschichte Jesu von Nazara in ihrer Verkettung mit dem Gesamtleben seines Volkes* (Zurich: Orell, Fussli & Co., 1867), 21. Cited by Theissen and Winter, *The Quest for the Plausible Jesus,* 266.

15. Adolf von Harnack, *What Is Christianity?* trans. Thomas Bailey Saunders (New York: Harper & Row, 1957), 16. Original title *Das Wesen des Christentums,* based on lectures delivered in 1899/1900. Cited in Theissen and Winter, *Quest,* 269.

16. Adolf Jülicher, "Die Religion Jesu und die Anfänge des Christentums bis zum Nicaenum," 42–131, *Die Kultur des Gegenwart,* vol. 1, sect. 4, *Geschichte der christlichen Religion,* ed. Paul Hinnenberg, 2d ed. (Berlin: Teubner, 1909), 58, 68. Cited in Theissen and Winter, *Quest,* 273.

17. Eduard Lohse, "Die Frage nach dem historischen Jesus in der gegenwärtigen neutestamentlichen Forschung," *Theologische Literaturzeitung* 87 (1962): 161–74, 168. Cited in Theissen and Winter, *Quest,* 283.

18. Theissen and Winter, *Quest,* 3.

19. Rudolf Bultmann, *Theology of the New Testament,* trans. Kendrick Grobel, Scribner Studies in Contemporary Theology (New York: Charles Scribner's Sons, 1951), 11.

20. See E. P. Sanders, *Paul and Palestinian Judaism: A Comparison of Patterns of Religion* (Philadelphia: Fortress Press, 1977), 33–59. His section, "The persistence of the view of Rabbinic religion as one of legalistic works-righteousness," is an excellent summary of the ways in which particular characteristics of Judaism are repeated in German scholarship, without any access to Jewish primary sources or Jewish historians or biblical interpreters, or even English writers, such as George Foote Moore, who challenged the prevailing Christian view of Judaism in "Christian Writers on Judaism," *Harvard Theological Review* 14 (1921): 197–254.

21. E. P. Sanders, *Jesus and Judaism* (London: SCM, 1985), 16.

22. James H. Charlesworth, *Jesus within Judaism: New Light from Exciting Archaeological Discoveries* (New York: Doubleday, 1988), 6. Cited in Theissen and Winter, *Quest*, 308.

23. Charlesworth, *Jesus within Judaism*, 167. Cited in Theissen and Winter, *Quest*, 308.

24. Bernard J. Lee, *The Galilean Jewishness of Jesus: Retrieving the Jewish Origins of Christianity*, vol. 1, *Conversation on the Road Not Taken* (New York: Paulist, 1988), 1:96. Cited in Theissen and Winter, *Quest*, 309.

25. John Dominic Crossan, "Divine Immediacy and Human Immediacy: Towards a New First Principle in Historical Jesus Research," *Semeia* 44 (1988): 125. Cited in Theissen and Winter, *Quest*, 309.

26. Theissen and Winter, *Quest*, 35.

27. Marcus J. Borg, "Reflections on a Discipline: A North American Perspective," in *Studying the Historical Jesus: Evaluations of the State of Current Research*, ed. Bruce D. Chilton and Craig A. Evans (Leiden: Brill, 1994), 26–27. Cited in Theissen and Winter, *Quest*, 315.

28. Borg, "Reflections on a Discipline."

29. See, for example, Marcus J. Borg, *Meeting Jesus Again for the First Time: The Historical Jesus and the Heart of Contemporary Faith* (San Francisco: HarperSanFrancisco, 1994), 47–58. In this popular, accessible, engaging book, Borg contrasts Jesus' compassion with the Pharisees' elitism and exclusivism in observing ritual purity laws. Borg knows the literature on early Judaism very well. He relies on Jacob Neusner's definition of the Pharisees at the time of Jesus. See my discussion on defining the Pharisees in chapter 3.

30. "The Telephone Pole Problem," *Homiletics* 16, no. 3 (May 2004): 23, 24.

31. Ibid., 23.

32. John W. Wimberly Jr., "Jesus: A Model of Tolerance or Intolerance?" *The Living Pulpit* 12, no.1 (January–March 2003): 28.

33. Joan Delaplane, "Is Tolerance Christian?" *The Living Pulpit* 12, no. 1 (January–March 2003): 21.

34. Walter J. Burghardt, "Tolerance: Christ and the Christian Preacher," *The Living Pulpit* 12, no. 1 (January–March 2003): 22, 23.

35. David P. Efroymson, "Jesus: Opposition and Opponents," *Within Context: Essays on Jews and Judaism in the New Testament*, ed. David P. Efroymson, et al. (Collegeville, Minn.: Liturgical, 1993), 102.

36. Clark M. Williamson, "Anti-Judaism in Process Christologies?" Available online at http://www.religion-online.org/showarticle.asp?title=24 92; accessed September 27, 2005.

37. Peter Hamilton, "Some Proposals for a Modern Christology," in

Process Philosophy and Christian Thought, ed. Delwin Brown, Ralph E. James, Jr. and Gene Reeves (Indianapolis: Bobbs-Merrill, l971), 365. Cited by Williamson, "Anti-Judaism in Process Christologies?" 7.

38. Ibid., 366.

39. W. Norman Pittenger, *Christology Reconsidered* (London: SCM, 1970), 72. Cited by Williamson, "Anti-Judaism in Process Christologies?" 8.

40. Ibid.

41. Lewis S. Ford, *The Lure of God: A Biblical Background for Process Theism* (Philadelphia: Fortress Press, 1978), 31. Cited by Williamson, "Anti-Judaism in Process Christologies?" 13.

42. Ibid.

43. John B. Cobb Jr., *The Structure of Christian Existence* (Philadelphia: Westminster, 1967), 110. Cited by Williamson, "Anti-Judaism in Process Christologies?" 14.

44. Ibid.

45. John B. Cobb Jr., *Christ in a Pluralistic Age* (Philadelphia: Westminster, 1975), 107. Cited by Williamson, "Anti-Judaism in Process Christologies?" 14.

46. Cobb, *The Structure of Christian Existence*, 142. Cited by Williamson, "Anti-Judaism in Process Christologies?" 14.

47. Schubert Ogden, *Christ without Myth: A Study Based on the Theology of Rudolf Bultmann* (New York: Harper & Brothers, 1961), 144. Cited by Williamson, "Anti-Judaism in Process Christologies?" 15.

48. Ibid., 143. Cited by Williamson, "Anti-Judaism in Process Christologies?" 16.

49. Williamson, "Anti-Judaism in Process Christologies?" 18.

50. Ibid.

51. Mary Boys, *Has God Only One Blessing? Judaism as a Source of Christian Self-Understanding* (New York: Paulist, 2000), 13.

52. Ibid., 297–98, n. 17.

53. See John Pawlikowski, *Christ in the Light of the Jewish-Christian Dialogue,* Studies in Judaism and Christianity (New York: Paulist, 1982), 64. In his chapter assessing current systematic theologies, Pawlikowski discusses the supersessionist tendencies in liberation Christologies, 59–75.

54. Jon Sobrino, *Christology at the Crossroads: A Latin American Approach,* trans. John Drury (Maryknoll, N.Y.: Orbis, 1978), 207.

55. Ibid., 209.

56. Jon Sobrino, *Jesus the Liberator: A Historical-Theological View of Jesus of Nazareth,* trans. Paul Burns (Maryknoll, N.Y.: Orbis, 1993), 168–70.

57. Ibid., 170–78.

58. Leonardo Boff, *Passion of Christ, Passion of the World: The Facts, Their Interpretation, and Their Meaning, Yesterday and Today*, trans. Robert R. Barr (Maryknoll, N.Y.: Orbis, 1987), 13. Cited in Boys, *Has God Only One Blessing?* 298, n. 22.

59. Boff, *Passion of Christ*, 195.

60. Marianne Grohmann, "Feminist Theology and Jewish-Christian Dialogue," trans. Astrid Foster. Available online at http://members.tripod.com/JCRelations/fem.html; accessed September 28, 2005. This article was first printed in the Austrian magazine *Dialog-Du Siach*.

61. See, for example, Elizabeth Gould Davis, *The First Sex* (New York: Putnam, 1971); Sheila D. Collins, *A Different Heaven and Earth* (Valley Forge, Pa.: Judson, 1974); Gerda Lerner, *The Creation of Patriarchy* (New York: Oxford University Press, 1986).

62. Leonard Swidler, "Jesus Was a Feminist," *The South East Asia Journal of Theology* 13, no. 1 (1971): 102–3.

63. Krister Stendahl, *The Bible and the Role of Women: A Case Study in Hermeneutics*, Facets (Philadelphia: Fortress Press, 1966), 26. Cited by Judith Plaskow, "Christian Feminism and Anti-Judaism," *Cross Currents* 28, no. 3 (Fall 1978): 307.

64. See Judith Hauptman, *Rereading the Rabbis: A Woman's Voice* (Boulder, Colo.: Westview, 1998).

65. Grohmann, "Feminist Theology and Jewish-Christian Dialogue," 2.

66. Boys, *Has God Only One Blessing?* 13.

67. Sermon delivered at a chapel service at United Theological Seminary of the Twin Cities, New Brighton, Minn., September 2004.

68. Keith A. Russell, "Why Does Someone Have to Win?" *The Living Pulpit* 12, no. 1 (January–March 2003): 16.

69. Barbara Brown Taylor, "Never-Ending Story," *The Christian Century* 120, no. 5 (March 8, 2003): 37.

70. Ibid.

3. The Pharisees and the Law

1. Krister Stendahl, "Introduction," in Leo Baeck, *The Pharisees and Other Essays* (New York: Schocken, 1966), xi.

2. Paul claims to be a Pharisee, but many think he rejected Pharisaism when he became a follower of Christ. See, for example, Alan Segal, *Paul the Convert: The Apostolate and Apostasy of Saul the Pharisee* (New Haven: Yale University Press, 1990). Acts presents Paul as a model Torah-observant Pharisee, but this portrayal serves the purpose of the author, a legitimation of Paul's mission. See Robert Brawley, *Luke-Acts and the Jews: Conflict, Apology, and Conciliation* (Atlanta: Scholars, 1987).

3. Hillel and Shammai were contemporaries of Jesus and represent two schools of interpretation of the Oral Torah. They represent lenient and more stringent legal opinions respectively.

4. Jacob Neusner, *Rabbinic Traditions about the Pharisees before 70* A.D. (Leiden: Brill, 1971).

5. Jacob Neusner, *From Politics to Piety: The Emergence of Pharisaic Judaism* (Englewood Cliffs, N.J.: Prentice-Hall, 1973).

6. Ellis Rivkin, *A Hidden Revolution: The Pharisees' Search for the Kingdom Within* (Nashville: Abindgon, 1978).

7. Neusner, *From Politics to Piety*, 146.

8. Josephus, *Jewish War*, trans. H. S. J. Thackeray, Loeb Classical Library (Cambridge, Mass.: Harvard University Press, 1976), 2:163.

9. Ibid., 2:166.

10. Josephus, *Jewish Antiquities,* trans. H. St. J. Thackeray, Loeb Classical Library (Cambridge, Mass.: Harvard University Press, 1976), 13:297–298.

11. Ibid., 18:12.

12. Ibid., 18:15.

13. Josephus, *Life*, trans. H. S. J. Thackeray, Loeb Classical Library (Cambridge, Mass.: Harvard University Press, 1976), 12.

14. Rivkin, *A Hidden Revolution*, 297.

15. Josephus, *Jewish War* 2:163. Rivkin objects to the term "sect" arguing that a better translation for *hairesus* is "party." He believes that "sect" implies a separation from the mainstream that does not define the description of the Pharisees.

16. Josephus, *Jewish Antiquities* 18:17.

17. Shmuel Safrai, "Oral Tora," in *The Literature of the Sages: Part One,* ed. Shmuel Safrai, Compendia Rerum Iudaicarum ad Novum Testamentum (Philadelphia: Fortress Press, 1987), 36.

18. Ibid., 60–65.

19. Anthony Saldarini, *Pharisees, Scribes, and Sadducees in Palestinian Society: A Sociological Approach,* second ed., Biblical Resource (Grand Rapids, Mich.: Eerdmans, 2001), 281, 282.

20. Ibid., 285, 283.

21. See the discussion in chapter 2.

22. Josephus uses this term for the Oral Torah. See *Jewish Antiquities* 13:297. So does Paul, in Gal. 1:14.

23. See *Mishnah* tractate *Pirke Avoth* 1:1, which traces the transmission of Torah back to Moses.

24. Luke Timothy Johnson, "The New Testament's Anti-Jewish Slander and the Conventions of Ancient Polemic," *Journal of Biblical Literature* 108, no. 3 (1989): 424–29.

25. See J. A. Ziesler, "Luke and the Pharisees," *New Testament Studies* 25 (1978–79): 146–56.

26. The word here, *dialogizomai*, means legal argument, debate; used elsewhere in Luke.

27. See *Mishnah* tractate *Yoma* 8:5-6. We exercise caution in assuming the laws codified in *Mishnah* relate to first-century customs. Some do and some do not. In this case there is no reason to think that the principle of observance was different than the one stated in *Yoma*.

28. Jacob Jervell, "The Law in Luke-Acts," in *Luke and the People of God: A New Look at Luke-Acts* (Minneapolis: Augsburg, 1972).

29. David Tiede, *Luke*, Augsburg Commentary on the New Testament (Minneapolis: Augsburg, 1988), 257. Tiede asserts that it is impossible to tell if these Pharisees are sincere in their desire to protect Jesus from harm. He notes that Jesus does not take their counsel.

30. Robert L. Brawley, *Luke-Acts and the Jews: Conflict, Apology, and Conciliation* (Atlanta: Scholars, 1987), 86.

31. Ibid., 105.

32. Mary Boys, *Has God Only One Blessing? Judaism as a Source of Christian Self-Understanding* (Paulist: New York, 2000), 189.

33. John W. Wimberly Jr., "Jesus: A Model of Tolerance or Intolerance?" *The Living Pulpit* 12, no. 1 (January–March, 2003): 28. This issue features articles on the subject of tolerance.

34. Keenan Kelsey, "A Good Day to Be a Receiver," Noe Valley Ministry Presbyterian Church, San Francisco; http://www.noevalleyministry.org /services.html; accessed October 26, 2003.

35. Joe Clifford, "The Mother Hen," Alpharetta Presbyterian Church, Alpharetta, Ga.; http://www.alpharettapres.com/mar_7,_2004.htm; accessed March 7, 2004.

36. Ibid., citing Edwin Friedman, *A Failure of Nerve: Leadership in the Age of the Quick Fix*, four audiotaped lectures (New York: Guilford, 1996).

37. Barbara K. Lundblad, "Personal, But Never Private," The Protestant Hour Sermon Index Page; http://www.day1.net/index.php5? view=transcripts &tid=279; accessed October 3, 2005.

38. Sermon delivered on the Seventh Sunday of Epiphany, St. Clement's Episcopal Church, St. Paul, Minn., February 23, 2003.

39. Ibid.

40. Saldarini, *Pharisees, Scribes, and Sadducees*, 275, 276.

41. Ibid.

42. William G. Stroop, "Getting Down and Dirty"; http://www .williamgstroop.com/Sermons/Year%20B/YrB-Pr17.htm; accessed October 3, 2005.

43. Ibid.

44. E. P. Sanders, "Jewish Association with Gentiles and Galatians 2:11-14," in *The Conversation Continues: Studies in Paul and John in Honor of*

J. Louis Martyn, ed. Robert T. Fortna and Beverly Roberts Gaventa (Nashville: Abingdon, 1990), 175.

45. *Yadaim* 3:5.

46. E. P. Sanders, *Jewish Law from Jesus to the Mishnah: Five Studies* (Philadelphia: Trinity Press International, 1990), 159.

47. Scott Salmon provided this quote from his teacher, Donald Verseput. Verseput's untimely death is a loss to his students and to New Testament scholarship.

48. Tim Hart-Anderson, "The Staying Power of Faith," based on Luke 7:36-50, Westminster Presbyterian Church, Minneapolis, Minn.; http://www.ewestminster.org/sermon.asp?id=411; accessed October 3, 2005.

49. Barbara Brown Taylor, "Living by the Word," *The Christian Century* 115, no. 8 (March 11, 1998): 257.

50. Unfortunately, she misrepresents the purity laws, relating them to hygiene, outcasts, and undesirable company.

51. Boys, *Has God Only One Blessing?* 188.

52. Sermon delivered on the Twelfth Sunday after Pentecost, St. Clement's Episcopal Church, St. Paul, Minn., August 31, 2003.

53. Barbara Brown Taylor, "Faith Matters," *The Christian Century* 121, no. 5 (March 9, 2004): 39.

4. The Gospel of John

1. Crossan made this comment during a reading and discussion of his book, *Who Killed Jesus? Exposing the Roots of Anti-Semitism in the Gospel Story of the Death of Jesus* (San Francisco: HarperSanFrancisco, 1995), at the Hungry Mind Bookstore, St. Paul, Minnesota, Spring 1996.

2. Barbara Brown Taylor, "Never-Ending Story," *The Christian Century* 120, no. 5 (March 8, 2003): 37.

3. Ibid.

4. Many leading Johannine scholars claim that the Fourth Gospel contains narratives from three different time periods following the death of Jesus. Even if one assigns material within the Gospel to different times, there is general consensus that the expulsion from the synagogue belongs to the final redaction of John.

5. J. Louis Martyn, *History and Theology in the Fourth Gospel*, New Testament Library, 2d ed. (Nashville: Abingdon, 1979).

6. David A. Reed, "The Expulsion from the Synagogue in John's Gospel—A New Perspective on Its Origins," paper presented at the Upper Midwest Society for Biblical Literature Meeting, St. Paul, Minnesota, April 2005.

7. Daniel Boyarin, "The *Ioudaioi* and the Prehistory of 'Judaism,'" in *Pauline Conversations on Context: Essays in Honor of Calvin J. Roetzel*, ed. Janice Capel Anderson, et al. (London: Sheffield Academic Press, 2002), 219.

8. Reed, "The Expulsion from the Synagogue," 1.

9. Ibid., 10.

10. Ibid., 19.

11. See, for example, Wayne A. Meeks, "The Man from Heaven in Johannine Sectarianism," *Journal of Biblical Literature* 91 (1972): 70. Meeks answers "yes." Raymond Brown disagrees. See Raymond E. Brown, *The Community of the Beloved Disciple: The Lives, Loves, and Hates of an Individual Church in New Testament Times* (New York: Paulist, 1979).

12. David Rensberger, *Johannine Faith and Liberating Community* (Philadelphia: Westminster, 1988), 27–28.

13. David G. Burke, "Translating *Hoi Ioudaioi* in the New Testament," *Explorations* 9, no. 2 (1995): 1.

14. Ibid. See page 4 of his essay for a table comparing several translations of verses citing *Ioudaioi*. See also Barclay M. Newman, "Making Peace between Jews and Gentiles," *Explorations* 10, no. 1 (1996): 7.

15. Joseph Blenkinsopp, "The Contemporary English Version: Inaccurate Translation Tries to Soften Anti-Judaic Sentiment," *Bible Review* 12 (October 1996): 42.

16. Gerard S. Sloyan, *John*, Interpretation (Atlanta: John Knox, 1988), xiv.

17. Ibid.

18. Sermon delivered on the Fourth Sunday in Lent, St. Clement's Episcopal Church, St. Paul, Minn., March 14, 1999.

19. Rensberger, *Johannine Faith and Liberating Community*, 60.

20. Sermon delivered on the First Sunday after Christmas, St. Clement's Episcopal Church, St. Paul, Minn., December 30, 2001.

21. Ibid., 136.

22. Rensberger, *Johannine Faith and Liberating Community*, 142.

23. Taylor, "Never-Ending Story," 37.

5. The Passion Narrative

1. Rabbi Barry Cytron made this comment in a panel discussion at Luther Seminary, St. Paul, Minn., shortly after the release of the movie, in March 2004. Rabbi Cytron occupies the J. B. Phillips Chair of Christian-Jewish Learning at the University of St. Thomas in St. Paul and St. John's University in Collegeville, Minn.

2. Vatican guidelines are available at several Web sites. See, for example, Leonard W. Swidler, with Gerard Sloyan, "The Passion of the Jew Jesus: Recommended Changes in the Oberammergau Passion Play after 1984," edited by Ingrid H. Shafer; http://ecumene.org/SHOAH/oberammer.htm; accessed October 5, 2005.

3. Cited in Barbara Brown Taylor, "Teaching Contempt," *The Christian Century* 121, no. 17 (August 24, 2004): 37.

4. Raymond Brown, *The Death of the Messiah: From Gethsemane to the Grave—A Commentary on the Passion Narratives in the Four Gospels* (New York: Doubleday, 1994).

5. John Dominic Crossan, *Who Killed Jesus? Exposing the Roots of Anti-Semitism in the Gospel Story of the Death of Jesus* (San Francisco: HarperSanFrancisco, 1995), 10.

6. Ibid., 35.

7. Brown, *The Death of the Messiah*, 383–97.

8. Michael Lerner, cited in Taylor, "Teaching Contempt," 37.

9. Calvin J. Roetzel, *The World That Shaped the New Testament* (Atlanta: John Knox, 1985), 16.

10. Josephus, *Jewish War*, trans. H. S. J. Thackeray, Loeb Classical Library (Cambridge, Mass.: Harvard University Press, 1976), 2:169–74.

11. Ibid., 2:175–177.

12. Roetzel, *The World That Shaped the New Testament*, 17.

13. Ellis Rivkin, *What Crucified Jesus? The Political Execution of a Charismatic* (Nashville: Abingdon, 1984), 33.

14. Josephus, *Jewish Antiquities*, trans. H. S. J. Thackeray, Loeb Classical Library (Cambridge, Mass.: Harvard University Press, 1976), 20: 197–200.

15. Ibid., 20:201–203.

16. Rivkin, *What Crucified Jesus?* 35.

17. Josephus, *Jewish War* 2:254–257.

18. Rivkin, *What Crucified Jesus?* 16–55.

19. Minneapolis *Star Tribune*, March 26, 2005, Faith and Values section.

20. Ibid.

21. Gerard Sloyan, *Why Jesus Died?* Facets (Minneapolis: Fortress Press, 2004). Sloyan cites several primary sources on the subject of crucifixion, 14–18.

22. Josephus, *Jewish War* 5:449–452.

23. John Stensvaag of blessed memory was professor of Old Testament at Luther Seminary in St. Paul, Minn.

24. Crossan, *Who Killed Jesus?* 1.

25. James Carroll, *Constantine's Sword: The Church and the Jews, a History* (New York: Houghton Mifflin, 2001), 297.

26. Sermon delivered on Good Friday, St. Clement's Episcopal Church, St. Paul, Minn., March 29, 2002.

27. David Tiede made this observation in a class lecture at Luther Seminary when I was a student in my first year, 1974. Obviously, it made an impression!

28. Oscar Romero, cited in an e-mail letter from Lutheran pastor and activist James Siefkes, in reference to the twenty-second anniversary of Romero's death, 2002.

29. Cited in Stephen J. S. Smith, "Foolishness," in *Preaching through the Year of Matthew: Sermons That Work*, vol. 10, ed. Roger Alling and David H. Schlafer (Harrisburg, Pa.: Morehouse, 2001), 51.

30. Barbara Anderson, "Liberation Theology," delivered April 15, 2001 (Easter Sunday), Pasadena Presbyterian Church, Pasadena, Calif.; http://www.ppc.net/sermons/text/04-15-01.html; accessed October 5, 2005.

31. Ibid.

32. Sermon delivered on Maundy Thursday, St. Clement's Episcopal Church, St. Paul, Minn., April 17, 2003.

33. See note 2 above. There are also several Web sites on the Oberammergau Play.

34. See, for example, an annotated "Johannine Passion Narrative," http://www.bc.edu/research/cjl/meta-elements/sites/partners/cbaa_seminar/Johannine_PassionNarrann.htm; accessed October 5, 2005. See also John T. Townsend, "A Liturgical Interpretation of Our Lord's Passion in Narrative Form" (New York: National Conference of Christians and Jews, 1977), http://www.bc.edu/research/cjl/meta-elements/sites/partners/cbaa_seminar/townsend_lit_int.htm; accessed October 21, 2005.

Conclusion

1. Barbara Brown Taylor, "Teaching Contempt," *The Christian Century* 121, no. 17 (August 24, 2004): 37.

2. Ibid.

Suggestions for Further Reading

Allen, Ronald J., and Clark M. Williamson. *Preaching the Gospels without Blaming the Jews*. Louisville: Westminster John Knox, 2004.

Boys, Mary C. *Has God Only One Blessing? Judaism as a Source of Christian Self-Understanding*. New York: Paulist, 2000.

Brawley, Robert. *Luke-Acts and the Jews: Conflict, Apology, and Conciliation*. Atlanta: Scholars, 1987.

Carroll, James. *Constantine's Sword: The Church and the Jews, a History*. New York: Houghton Mifflin, 2001.

Cohen, Shaye J. D. *The Beginnings of Jewishness: Boundaries, Varieties, Uncertainties*. Hellenistic Culture and Society. Berkeley: University of California Press, 1999.

Crossan, John Dominic. *Who Killed Jesus? Exposing the Roots of Anti-Semitism in the Gospel Story of the Death of Jesus*. San Francisco: HarperSanFrancisco, 1995.

Efroymson, David P., Eugene J. Fisher, and Leon Klenicki, eds. *Within Context: Essays on Jews and Judaism in the New Testament*. Collegeville, Minn.: Liturgical, 1993.

Fredriksen, Paula, and Adele Reinhartz, eds. *Jesus, Judaism, and Christian Anti-Judaism: Reading the New Testament after the Holocaust*. Louisville: Westminster John Knox, 2002.

Holmgren, Fredrick C. *The Old Testament and the Significance of Jesus: Embracing Change—Maintaining Christian Identity*. Grand Rapids: Eerdmans, 1999.

Jervell, Jacob. "The Law in Luke-Acts." In *Luke and the People of God: A New Look at Luke-Acts*. Minneapolis: Augsburg, 1972.

Johnson, Luke Timothy. "The New Testament's Anti-Jewish Slander and the Conventions of Ancient Polemic." *Journal of Biblical Literature* 108, no. 3 (1989): 424–29.

Juel, Donald H. *The Gospel of Mark*. Interpreting Biblical Texts. Nashville: Abingdon, 1999.

Overman, J. Andrew. *Church and Community in Crisis: The Gospel according to Matthew.* Valley Forge, Pa.: Trinity Press International, 1996.

Rensberger, David. *Johannine Faith and Liberating Community.* Philadelphia: Westminster, 1988.

Roetzel, Calvin J. *The World That Shaped the New Testament.* Atlanta: John Knox, 1985.

Saldarini, Anthony J. *Pharisees, Scribes, and Sadducees in Palestinian Society: A Sociological Approach.* Biblical Resources. 2d ed. Grand Rapids: Eerdmans, 2001.

Sloyan, Gerard S. *Why Jesus Died.* Facets. Minneapolis: Fortress Press, 2004.

Theissen, Gerd, and Dagmar Winter. *The Quest for the Plausible Jesus: The Question of Criteria.* Trans. Eugene Boring. Louisville: Westminster John Knox, 2002.

Tiede, David. *Luke.* Augsburg Commentary on the New Testament. Minneapolis: Augsburg, 1988.

Index of
Names and Subjects

Index of
Ancient Sources